Lois Lovina Murray

Incidents of frontier life

In two parts

Lois Lovina Murray

Incidents of frontier life
In two parts

ISBN/EAN: 9783337147969

Printed in Europe, USA, Canada, Australia, Japan

Cover: Foto ©ninafisch / pixelio.de

More available books at **www.hansebooks.com**

LOIS. L. MURRAY.

INCIDENTS

OF

Frontier Life.

IN TWO PARTS.

CONTAINING RELIGIOUS INCIDENTS AND MORAL COMMENT, RELATING TO VARIOUS OCCURRENCES, EVILS OF INTEMPERANCE, AND HISTORICAL AND BIOGRAPHICAL SKETCHES.

BY MRS. LOIS L. MURRAY.

WRITTEN FROM PERSONAL EXPERIENCE AND ANCESTRAL ACCOUNT OR CERTAIN KNOWLEDGE, IN THE YEAR 1878.

GOSHEN, INDIANA:
EV. UNITED MENNONITE PUBLISHING HOUSE.
1880.

PREFACE.

From a sense of the tender mercy and love of our heavenly Father, I have desired to write some of the consolations of grace; and have felt that it were ingratitude not thus to do. Some acquaintances and friends in the state of Kansas, remarked to me, that I ought to write some account of my "Frontier Life" in that State. And as earthly treasures have seemed to vanish from my view, and many of the cares of life with the same, I have thought proper to offer as a memento some of the observations and remembrances of life, commencing with an authentic account of the first settlement of Granville, Ohio, in which my ancestors have acted a part; then I have followed with remembrances of childhood, and incidents of the same, and have spoken without enlargement on any detail, but have given mere facts without variation.

I have sketched a little along through maturer life, and have detailed some accounts of the Indians and, the dangers and trials of my frontier life. I have spoken of grasshoppers and drouths, with a sketch of some things which might be classed under the head of Dangers and Trials.

I have made mention of some serious evils, which have come under my notice, and have made some comment on a variety of those things which have occurred within my notice. I have spoken of friends and broken ties, of the uncertainty of earthly things, and of a home in heaven.

Also of the progress and improvements of civilization; and closed with a journey on the cars, and some additional remarks; and if anything beneficial to anyone has been said, to Him that holdeth the stars in his right hand, be all the praise.

CONTENTS.

PART FIRST.

	CHAPTER.
A Colony.	1
In Rhyme, the Babe, the Home.	2
Dusky Visions, the Wolves.	3
The Sugar Camp.	4
Rest in a Tree.	5
A Bride.	6
A Feast.	7
Infancy.	8
My Father.	9
A Dream, a Text.	10
A Fight.	11
Left to her Fate.	12
The Slave of Rum.	13
Poor Man, I will give you Food.	14
A Pledge.	15
Grandmother's Story.	16
A Protracted Meeting.	17
Heavenly View.	18
A Dream.	19
The Swearer.	20
Returning from the Orchard.	21
When Fifteen Years of Age.	22

CONTENTS.—PART FIRST.

A Convention	23
A Child, a Jewel	24
The Trumpet Sound	25
Going Home, the Christian	26
A Sleigh-ride, a Wish	27
Christian Converse, Experience	28
Removal; Sketches by the Way	29
My Eldest Brother, a Rest	30
Providences, Afflictions, a Sacred Charge	31
Dear Father	32
A Sister on California Shores	33

PART SECOND.

	CHAPTER.
On the Cars, on the Boat	1
A Great Pet, a Black Cook	2
An Explosion	3
Dark Stairs	4
In Kansas	5
The First Indians	6
Cabin Home	7
Two Squaws	8
We Counted Seventy-five, and still they Came	9
In Iowa, Much Loss, Return, Buffaloes	10
Afflictions	11
A Dark Cloud, an Adventure	12
A Prairie Fire and Loss	13
A Poor Indian,	14
Degredation.	15
A Floor of Rock	16
An Indian, a Whip	17
The Squaws: "Give me that Cup."	18
The Indian Lullaby	19
They Wanted Whiskey. Stratigem, the Wicked	20
Chasing Wolves	21
Mr. Gray Coat	22
An Invitation, a Sabbath-school	23
Reading Sermons, Singing, Celebration	24
No Machinery, Heavy Toil	25

CONTENTS.—PART SECOND.

	CHAPTER.
Prairie Fire, God's Help	26
What we had for Food	27
He Went to Mill, Eleven Days Absent	28
In all our Walks and Labors Happy	29
Through a Snow-bank and got Wood	30
Red Paint, War Songs	31
Cedar Creek, Snow Storm	32
Four Savages	33
Met the Cannon's Roar	34
Doleful Lamentations	35
A Journey, a Powwow, and Burial	36
Texas and Mexican Trains. A Farce	37
A Pair of Moccasins	38
"Sister, Please Give me a Cup of Water."	39
Dried in Indian Style	40
He Came for Protection	41
They had Ashes on Their Heads	42
Four Savages Pulled him, From his Horse	43
A Train Robbed	44
A Stolen Animal	45
An Indian Feast	46
Antelope and Turkeys	47
Scalps of Enemies	48
A Flight From Savages	49
Savage Indians, a Race for Life	50
On a Stormy Sea, Testimony	51
Mr. G., Flight, Loss, and Danger	52
The Threat, the Conclusion	53
The Soldiers, the Indians	54
The Walk, the Mission	55
Pious Council, Wooden Shoes	56
A Dream, an Organization	57
Dear Mary, a Minister, a Quarterly Meeting	58

	CHAPTER.
Captain E. F. Abbott Killed	59
Afflictions. Conference sent a Preacher	60
Family Afflictions. Brother F. and Daughter	61
Grasshoppers, Flight from Indians	62
Severe Winter, Loss	63
Cultivation, Drouths, Grasshoppers	64
Mrs. Green's Story	65
Prairie Fire, Distressing Scene	66
Sense of Duty, The Sick	67
Four Savages. "Where is White Man."	68
Five Indians, Stolen Horses	69
Six Serpents	70
The Children's Fright	71
A Texas Ox, Danger	72
Indian Johnson, A Wild Pony, Indians	73
Milling Expedition. Mr. Gibson	74
Sister Brown, a Letter, Poetry	75
A Minister's Visit, a New Dwelling	76
A Broken Tie, Mary's Death	77
My Children's Loss, a Railroad, Boarders	78
A Texan, Ruffians at Newton	79
An Impression, a Sound, a Skeleton	80
Trials: House in Flames	81
An Absent Son, Freezing to Death	82
Grasshoppers, Losses, a Visit, our Relatives, a Terrible Visitation. A Dying Charge, An Acquaintance	83
An Adieu, Kansas Home	84
Alone Again. Heroism, Uncivility	85
She Changed her Name. Patrimony	86
Afflictions, Change of Residence	87
Within the Cars, Observations	88
A Lady, Union Flag, Penitentiary	89
At Mother's Home in Goshen	90

CONTENTS.—PART SECOND.

	CHAPTER.
A Journey	91
New Country	92
The Reckless	93
Visiting the Sick, Religion	94
The Prayer of Faith	95
A Guide	96

PART FIRST.

CHAPTER I.—A COLONY.

One morning in the year 1807, a company of thirty families, in New England, near the line of Connecticut and Massachusetts, citizens of the towns of Granville and Granby, were seen bidding their friends and neighbors a long adieu.

They then entered their vehicles, and turned their faces westward, firm with the spirit of enterprise and hope, as to a home in central Ohio, which was then a wilderness, inhabited by roving tribes of Indians; also the abode of the turkey, deer, panther, bear, and wolf, and covered with heavy timber, very unlike the prairies of our more western lands.

As these devoted emigrants moved onward, o'er hill and valley, mountain or river, they often halted to prepare the hasty repast, and allow their wearied teams to regale themselves with food and rest; and when the preparations of the hour were over, thanksgivings resounded to the God of all grace and blessings, as they remembered the divine command, to be thankful; and when the shades of night fell around them, the voice of a beloved pastor was heard on the evening air: returning thanks for preservations during the day, and supplicating the blessing of Almighty God on the slumbers of the little flock of wearied travelers; and when the golden rays of light illumed the horizon around them, with the divine blessing of Providence, they pressed onward.

Pastor and school teacher, parents, youths, and little children, all chasing the wild scenery, singing, conversing, and listening to the wild echoes.

(The colony above mentioned stopped every Sabbath during their journey; and their minister delivered them an address from the revealed will of God, and instructed the youth of the company in the form of Sabbath school.)

CHAPTER II.—IN RHYME. THE BABE. THE HOME.

And now a rhyme within these columns I will pen.
A little sleeping babe, within a covered willow basket lay,
Which to the wagon bows was firmly bound;
And swaying to and fro, the child rocked to sleep;
But as a mountain high they climbed,
The coupling of the carriage disengaged became.
When backward rolling, quickly overturned;
Then anxious parents hastily sought their child.
They found it, still with peaceful slumbers blest.
That babe, a woman now of seventy years,
My mother I do call.
But to my story now I turn, and trace
Those emigrants to their new found home.
There behold them, on the ground
Now called Granville, Licking county, Ohio.
Then a friendly brother's help was given,
Till all that colony a domicile could call their own;
And then, unitedly a church and school house,
All in one they raised.
That colony of Presbyterian order
Yet what matters it, by what name
Here on earth we are called,

If that new name, which only they can know
Who do receive, be ours:
A ticket, or a title to that blest home,
Beyond the etherial blue.
But lo! consumption followed with a stealthy tread,
And laid its chilling grasp on one,
Beloved by all that little band.
The junior, *Samuel Everiett named:
Colonial contracts, his employment was to fill
His pen he held, as long as failing strength allowed,
Then another held the pen,
While he instructions gave.
But oh! death pressed him on apace;
And then the weeping partner he did cheer,
And bade her meet him in the better land.
"My children," he cried.
"So live, that you may meet your Father,
When this short life is done:
Where sorrow never enters.
But my dear babe—hold her near,
That I may a father's blessing give,
While on her head my hand I lay.
Oh! Father, God, I pray thee bless my child,
And guide her to the realms of endless day.
There may these dear ones meet,
In one unbroken band, when time with them is o'er:

---

*Samuel Everiett bought the land where Granville, Ohio, is located, for a New England colony, and transacted the business of the same, till death closed the scene,

But Oh! the angels call, I to my Savior go
Adieu, loved ones, adieu!"
Oh! see the elder sire, the father, and grand-father,
While he bows submissive near, his marble child.
He cries, "My Father, God, thy will be done.
A little longer here I stay, then I will meet
My angel child in heaven above!"
He stayed eleven years more, and then
The youngest grandchild called and said:
"I go to that bright land where angels dwell.
Be faithful to the truth and right,
And I request thee, dearest child, to learn those
    blessed lines :

    'Ashamed of Jesus, just as soon.
    Let midnight be ashamed of noon.
    No, when I blush, be this my shame.
    That I no more revere His name.

    'Ashamed of Jesus, sooner far,
    Let evening blush to own a star.
    'Tis midnight with my soul till He,
    Bright Morning Star, bid darkness flee.'"

He no longer could converse, for by the icy hand
Of death, his voice was hushed ;
And then the pearly gates of the celestial City,
Opened wide, to let the ransomed one
With all the holy angels join.
And as we near the gates of heaven stand,
To watch the ransomed enter, Oh! let us turn
And look, for there are wandering ones

Still on the boistrous sea of life,
The widow and the fatherless:
Sustaining grace and help the widow's God affords;
For with eight children, left in country new,
The youngest only eighteen months had numbered;
When like a lonely bird without a mate,
The little ones unfledged, the widow lone,
With toils incessant, never seemed to tire.
The distaff she did hold,
And wool and flax transformed to yarn and cloth,
Her family did cloth.

CHAPTER III. DUSKY VISIONS. THE WOLVES.

But were there not some things, to fright her unfledged birds?
O yes, and one dark night a pet calf cried
Most bitterly. She said "I will go and see."
But to her dress, two children hung and cried,
"Oh! mother stay."
And on the morrow, all that of their pet remained,
Was just its hide rolled up.
The bears had carried all else far away.
But hark! indian wars in progress are,
And oft this family forbear throughout the night
    to sleep,
As dusky visions, both in real and in fancy meet.
The friendly indian hides his gun.
While to the cabin he repairs.
But lo! one night an indian sentinal stood,
With hatchet on his shoulder raised,
Glittering in the moonlight beams.
They watched all night;
But in the morning, lo! a lofty stump,
With spider web and dew upon the top.
After a time more peace did reign, and less of fear;

Then a little girl was seen, her mother's house to
 leave,
A sister's home to find.
Across the woods with hasty steps she flew,
Till suddenly, three large dogs she spied--
She stopped and scarcely dared to draw a breath.
For oh! those dogs might harm ;
But on they sped, the harmless deer to find ;
Then the child with speed before untold,
Her sister's home did gain :
But hark! the wolves her track had found ;
And to the house they came and round it howled.

CHAPTER IV.—THE SUGAR CAMP.

And when the time to make the maple sugar came,
Two children in the woods all night remained.
They watched the fire— the syrup down to sugar
    boiled.
A tent was spread, and all was closed around;
But just a door, near which a fire was built;
And when a growling bear they heard,
Or prowling wolf around,
They did the fire-brands throw, and heaped
More fuel on their fires, to fright the wild away.
Sometimes the mother came with light in hand;
And oft the shell-bark hickory torch,
More safe their pathway made,
Until their mother's house they gained.

CHAPTER V. REST IN A TREE.

One day a man came to their home and said:
Last night I took my rest in the branches of a tree;
For when from neighbor's house I late returned,
The glaring eyes, and snapping teeth around,
Did tell me you had better get from off the ground;
And in the morning I could see,
The hungry wolves had knawed the bark,
All round the bottom of my tree.

CHAPTER VI. A BRIDE.

But now enough of this, we will other thoughts
    engage ;
And while we entertain, may we instruction find.
The widow Everiett her eight children reared ;
Till in maturer years they found their mates.
And perched within their own dear homes.
Just seventeen summers o'er, the youngest child
    had passed.
When she, a blushing bride did stand ;
And while God's blessing, their pastor did implore.
Her hand was held by him.
With whom for many years, life's paths she trod.
The bride-groom, I. F. Abbott from New England
Had come and won his bride ;
And *I, their eldest child, do pen these lines.

---

*The original name of the writer was Lois Lovina Abbott, born March 3d, 1826.

CHAPTER VII.—A FEAST.

And when fifteen years more had fled,
I to an uncle's house did go:
My grandmother and her eight children saw,
And their companions too,
All seated at one table, with grandmother at the
    head;
And with the rest, a minister of God,
Who thanks returned to the almighty Giver of all
    good
And truly bountiful and nice was all:
We cannot here enumerate so much,
For turkey, pie, and cake, was only just a part:
And when the bounteous table rearranged be-
    came,
Many cousins side by side, with each
A cup of sparkling water standing by their plate;
And ministers with lifted hand God's blessing
    claimed.
This visit o'er, they in carriage procession
To another dwelling went:
The cousins at another uncles home arrived,
Their parents there, a feast, again they found pre-
    pared;

But oh! they parted, in such numbers.
Ne'er to meet again;
And that dear mother, who for more than forty
    years,
A widow's pathway trod,
Has went to meet her loved companion, long ago;
And of her children four have passed the pearly
    gates,
And four more waiting stand.
On Jordan's brink.
And of those cousins who with sparkling eyes and
    glowing cheeks,
The family feasts adorned.
A few have passed away;
While others still are left to tread these mortal
    shores;
But are their names all written in the Book of
    Life?
A part that witness have, which Enoch did possess:
And oh! that all who mortal are,
Might of salvation's current drink.
That they might thirst no more.
A Savior's smiles, a Father reconciled.
A Christ within the soul a faith how sweet.

CHAPTER VIII. INFANCY.

And now I will to infancy return,
And there a mother's smile,
While on her child she looked I greet;
And then my little chair I drew aside,
And by it bowed, to say my infant prayer.
But disobedience and self-will in Adam's race is
      surely found:
And up the steps so very high and steep I climed,
And hid behind the door, till lady left the room;
Then thought I would do the same,
And one step taken, down I rolled.
The next I knew, I lay on my father's lap,
Like a helpless babe,
Whilst father wiped blood from off my face.
And now let us of riper years a lesson take,
And ne'er our heavenly Father disobey,
For sin brings sorrow every where;
But if we are led and helped by God's own hand,
We will safely tread this rough world through.

CHAPTER IX. MY FATHER.

While seated in my father's arms, he told his little
Girl of Jesus, who for sinners died on Calvary;
For me, yes even me, his little child;
Then I wept, but they were precious tears;
So much of sympathy for him who died for me.
A school teacher boarded at my father's house,
And very young I learned to read;
But little follies I remembered, and bad examples
    saw.

CHAPTER X.—A DREAM. A TEXT.

One night I thought the judgment day had come,
And tried from God to hide;
Then I dreamed again that God and ministers
  followed me,
As I from them did run;
But soon one picked me up,
And in his arms he carried me, a little child.
Soon after this I sat upon a school-house bench,
And heard a pale patient minister of God pronounce these words:
"Come unto me, all ye that heavy laden are,
And I will give you rest."
Now if you will read the three last verses
Of the eleventh chapter of St. Matthew,
You will have all the text.
To a Sabbath-school I went, and there received
  nice good books,
Which did in my young mind the same inspire;
And in the chamber all alone with God,
My little hands before me clasped,
I prayed and know that Jesus heard.
When i had learned to write,
To my mother I a letter gave;

And within it I had wrote, "Oh! Mother dear.
To me you have been kind, and for me done
  much:
I thank thee, and may I be ever kind to thee."
I ran to hide, but mother called me back, and said,
A letter write and to your grandmother it shall
  be sent.

CHAPTER XL.--A FIGHT.

One day in a porch that was just pailed around,
I stood and saw drunken men in the street;
With clothing torn and stained with blood,
Like beasts in human form—
They struck, and bit, and gouged each others eyes;
And one was nearly blind the remainder of his life.
My mother came into that porch,
And little sister standing by, said, "Oh! ma,
Do not those men know that God can see?"
But ah! they were blinded by alcohol,
And little knew, but just to fight.
How bitterly by satan led, his weapon firey alcohol.

CHAPTER XII. LEFT TO HER FATE.

Into a store I went, there a woman sat already
    drunk,
And still for whiskey begged:
"Oh let me have just one glass more."
No wonder that a child
A sight so dismal would remember.
But this was not the last, of that woman to be told:
For once she took her little babe,
And horse-back went to town:
The father sought the babe, and found it by the
    road—
The horse was feeding near;
And drunken mother, partly in a mud-pond lay!
The father took the babe,
And left the drunken woman to her fate.

CHAPTER.—XIII THE SLAVE OF RUM.

The past would not suffice,
The slave must go again :
As she from town returned,
Whild passing through a woods,
She fell upon the ground—dead drunk :
Then wolves were seen to cover something up:
And when two persons went to see what the
    wolves had found,
There was Mrs. D. all covered up with leaves.
When they went to take the woman home,
Near twenty wolves were coming round
They shot and robbed the hungry wolves.
Perhaps you say, "They robbed the wolves too
    much!"
And oh! how base and low :
And yet the truth has not half been told!
For oh! the misery intemperance brings on such
    a family
We should not taste the poisonous cup,
Lest the serpent's fangs be fastened on our souls.
May God our country save,
From all that blasts, and blights, for Jesus' sake.

CHAPTER XIV. –I WILL GIVE YOU FOOD.

I saw one, who was called a tavern-keeper,
Kick an old man, with silvery locks,
Off from his porch;
Then whipped him with a heavy whip,
And knocked his head upon the ground;
Then threw a bucket of water on him as he lay.
The tavern-keeper had got the old man's money
That was all he cared.
My mother called across the way:
"Mr. M., if you will come to my back door,
I will give you tea and food.
He crawled upon his hands and knees, across the
 street.
And after eating, soberness returned;
Then the good advice my mother gave,
Was much and thankfully received,
While tears rolled down his face,
On a temperance pledge he wrote his name,
And never was drunk again.
Did Jesus come, sinners to save?
Oh! yes, the vilest of the vile.

CHAPTER XV.—A PLEDGE.

A young man fifteen years of age.
A temperance pledge took round our town,
And children over six, and under fourteen signed
    the pledge:
And a weekly temperance class was held.
Our leader prayed Almighty God to bless,
Then asked each their mind on temperance to
    speak.
A reform, was soon brought round.
And now that town, is for piety and temperance
    famed.

CHAPTER XVI.—GRANDMOTHER'S STORY.

I well remember the countenance of my aged grandmother;
Fair almost like a child.
Her hair had blossomed for the grave.
And oft when wintry winds the snow drifts piled,
She out the window looked and sighed then said
"Oh how my heart aches for the suffering poor.
One night when in Connecticut I dwelt
The wind was whistling round the snow drifts high.
I heard a scream for help—then it died away.
I called my family to hark!
We heard a call, twice or thrice,
But whither should we look or go.
A sleepless night I passed.
When daylight came, deep search was made,
And in a bank of snow, a woman's corpse was found;
Her frozen arms, a frozen babe, incircled round!"
The serpent alcohol had crazed her husband's brain,
And he had drove his hapless wife out in the howling storm;

And oh! the agony of remorse,
That must have filled the drunkard's soul,
When reason had usurped its throne.
That drunken husband, once a lovely child had
    been,
But oh! the dreadful work, the spoiler had done.
Oh! mothers dear, may God forbid that you
The dreadful work should see—a ruined son!
And oh! dear youth, temptation shun,
And ever do the right;
And may God keep your souls forever pure.
Much there is that we have heard or seen in later
    years,
That might be told of dread intemperance;
But this the present may suffice,
And on we pass to watch the swelling waves;
Our life a floating bark which Jesus saves.

CHAPTER XVII.—A PROTRACTED MEETING.

When nine years o'er my head to eternity had
    fled away,
My parents changed their residence,
And five miles distant went to dwell.
Soon a protracted meeting in that vicinity was
    held,
And in a new large barn.
A platform for ministers was reared.
God, through clay, did speak to those seated
    round.
The good seed did fall on some rich soil,
And upward grew to the glory of God's name.
"A society was formed, and when dear friends
Took their seats along the line,
I thought I would like with them to go to heaven.
I went forward and cast my lot with them.
An aged minister went round and clasped each
    friendly hand,
And when he came to me, he cried.
'Glory to God, is there another here to bring a
    child to God?"

On a full breeze for heaven we sailed,
And when to and from the house of prayer we
 went,
We almost seemed to walk the golden streets.
But only as a seeker of rich pearls I stood,
And sought our God alone three times a day,
Back of my father's orchard on the green,
Where none but God could see.
More instructions I needed in the way of life.

---

*The meeting here mentioned was held by the Protestant Methodist Church of which the writer was a member eight years and afterward became associated with the M. E. Church of which she was a member thirty-five years, and February 1879 she was indentified with the United Mennonite Church.

CHAPTER XVIII.—HEAVENLY VIEW.

One night from my sleep I waked,
And tears were rolling down my face.
Our dream was this: Into a room I entered,
And our Lord, the blessed Christ so very fair,
Was seated in the center,
To whom I did approach.
His countenance so wondrous light—
His smile how glorious sweet.
At his feet I fell: With his hand he raised me up.
Then I awoke: tears rolled like torrents down my
    face.
While that sweet vision of the lovely Christ,
Has all my life close on my footsteps seemed to
    tread.
The lovely Christ the blessed one—but language
    fails.
The glorious bridegroom his church doth love,
Which he hath bought with his precious blood;
And of that church triumphant,
May we make one for Jesus' sake.
But we thought religion was not a dream,
And with the poet still I said:

> "Oh! tell me that my worthless name
>   Is graven on thy hands.
> Show me some promise in thy book
>   Where my salvation stands."

I felt too vile for aught
But to throw myself on the ground,
And there with deep humility
Bedew the earth with tears.
I rose from prayer.
The golden sun just at the close of day,
Looked beautiful that hour;
But on one side a dark bundle seemed to rest,
And it was said to me,
"Your sins are all on Jesus laid,
The Sun of Righteousness."
I stood and praised the Lord
All things round me seemed to do the same:
The trees, the birds, the velvet earth,
While I said, "Glory be to God,
Blessed be thy holy name;"
And soon in union social meeting I rose and said,
"The precious pearl I have found;"
And with the poet I could say,

> "'Tis love that drives my chariot wheels,
>   And death must yield to love."

That was a happy meeting,
And all was warmth, life and praise.

Time onward passed for months all a sweet
 peace.
Three times a day, I went
Back of father's orchard alone to pray.
While bowed upon the ground,
My Savior on the cross by faith I saw,
While I looked and tears were on my face.
I spoke these words more times than I can tell:
"Oh blessed Jesus, blessed Lord."

CHAPTER XIX.—A DREAM.

One night I dreamed I stood upon a sea of ice,
Which cracked and broke;
And as I into the water sank, I upward looked
 and cried,
"Glory, glory, be to God, I am going home."
And very full of joy was I,
At the sweet thought of heaven.
After a time temptations came,
Then I would not eat one mouthful of pleasant
 food.
If a motion of sin within my soul I found,
And as a hart upon a mountain
Thirsts for cooling streams,
So did my soul thirst for the living God.

CHAPTER XX.—THE SWEARER.

One day I heard a lady say,
She had seen an aged man who enjoyed
The perfect love of God through Christ.
The aged man was happy, and faithful everywhere.
With his son he did reside.
Men came there to work.
One was angry, and swearing too.
But the elderly man walked near.
While tears rolled down his withered face,
He said, "oh! do not swear—
You might die before the sun shall set."
Then the swearer said with oaths upon his tongue,
"I will live as long as any here."
They went to work—but in an hour returned.
Bearing the swearer back—a corpse!
A limb had fallen from a tree
And struck him on the head—
He fell doubled to the earth, a mangled corpse.
Sinners do not presume upon God's mercy
Or his rod defy,
Or you may meet a dreadful doom.

CHAPTER XXI.—RETURNING FROM THE ORCHARD.

Now back to the aged pious man we will look,
And think how much we wished
The same grace might rest on such a one as I.
One day when returning from the orchard,
Where I had been to pray,
There was a wondrous power rested on unworthy
    me;
Much like Stephen, heaven seemed opened in the
    sky.
There I thought I saw our blessed Lord;
And angels round him bowed.
This vision o'er us passed,
And oh! the bliss unuterable,
Which did our being fill—
It was more than we could ever speak or ever tell;
But silence heightened heaven.

CHAPTER XXII.—WHEN FIFTEEN YEARS OF AGE.

But here we cannot stay—the moments fled.
The hours have pased.
The eldest of six children, we
The younger ones loved.
At home, or school, we thought
We would the time redeem,
And do with all our might
What ere we could.
Our studies all were mixed with prayer.
We did not our God forget.
Careless mirth and vanity we shuned;
Those things we could not love—
We had higher sweeter joys.
Our Bible class at Sabbath-school we prized.
And *Pilgrim's Progress* loved to read.
We could fathom all, God's Holy Spirit taught
    us there.
When fifteen years of age,
We taught a district school;
And ever that school with prayer commenced.
The committee said, that we should teach

Eight hours each day of school.
To this we did attend,
And faithful was in all,
The time we taught, within Ohio ground.
Of months we number twenty-four;
And just the same in Indiana range,
And ten in Kansas.
Which doth make in all, fifty-eight months,
Or nineteen quarters and one month;
And more than this, we every other Saturday,
Within that time did teach,
Which now is not the tune.

CHAPTER XXIII.—A CONVENTION.

The summer of 1841,
Nearly all the people throughout the land,
To a political convention went,
That in mount Vernon,
Knox Co., Ohio, was held.
All the young ladies in our community,
And I with them was dressed in white;
With ribbons blue for sash;
And on the neck the same.
In one large vehicle we rode,
And just in front,
On conveyance similar to ours,
A band of music played;
But I will not tell all,
For there was much display.
When there arrived, we found
Several thousand people on the ground;
And general Harrison too;
But near the lecture ground,
Men upon a wagon stood,
And while there steeds went round the throng,
With ax and mallet they split rails.

As hard as they could ply,
To show how Harrison had toiled.
And there were log cabins, built on wheels,
And by horses drawn around,
With union flags upon the top,
To show that Harrison had in a cabin lived.
We had a seat upon the lecture ground,
But lecture o'er, a feast, all free was spread,
To feed the numbers there.
And more than this, a roasted ox,
That looked nicely dressed,
And all in form,
Upon a wagon stood;
And flags were on its horns,
And while the team went round,
Men cut the meat from roasted ox,
And said, "here, here, take some,"
A cannon men were firing,
Burst and killed one man.
That man had been one who drank too much,
Of that he never should have touched.
He left a wife, and several little ones.
General Harrison to that widow went,
Before he left that town;
He gave his note for five hundred,
To that widow to be paid;
And with this note she bought a home,
Ere that time a home she ne'er possessed.

Though Harrison the presidential seat obtained.
He quickly passed from earth;
And I heard one say,
 "Perhaps our nation loved, and honored him so much,
That they robbed God of love, and honor too."
Surely time will pass away.
With all its forms of gaudy show.

CHAPTER XXIV.—A CHILD, A JEWEL.

See that little boy on the street,
With bare feet this wintry day.
Does not God within that little soul a jewel see?
But there come boys, with socks and boots,
All nice on their feet.
They say, "For shame a barefoot boy."
Then one stamps the little naked toes,
And make him cry with pain.
But ah! the needy boy may rise, whilst others fall;
And if he should not fill a presidential seat,
He may with God in glory dwell;
And there he will be clothed in angel's dress
White and fair.
Now dear child,
Jesus can wash you clean from sin—
He for you has died;
He has promised wisdom if you ask,
And he will surely give.

CHAPTER XXV.—THE TRUMPET SOUND.

Hark! while we pass along,
We hear the gospel trumpet sound;
"Free grace." Amazing sweet,
But lo! through instruments of clay, our God
 doth speak;
And 'tis the peals of mighty truth,
God's Holy Spirit's sword, the word of God.
But oh! there are some who God resist and sin
 pursue.
Dreadful thought! they on the way to ruin run.
Oh! hark, the sound eternity! eternity!
In darkness wrapt, and far from God—
A guilty soul.
We hear a skeptic cry, Oh! for a day,
Oh! for a single hour,
Although an age too little were,
For the much I have to do;
But ah! that one has passed away,
In despair he closed his eyes in death.
Oh! death, how dreadful must thy summons be,
To those that are at ease in their possessions.
How the foe like a staunch murderer,
Pursues the guilty soul through every lane of life;

She runs to every avenue and shrieks for help,
But shrieks in vain;
For down the verge she is pressed—
To endless ruin.

CHAPTER XXVI.—GOING HOME, THE CHRISTIAN.

But what a contrast now I see;
For standing by a Christian's bed,
I heard her say, while at her hands she looked,
And saw that in her veins
The purple current would no longer flow,
Dying is like going a friend to see,
And a pleasant visit make.
Then with peace and joy she said,

> "Jesus can make a dying bed
>   Feel soft, as downy pillows are;
> While on his breast I lean my head,
>   And breathe my life out sweetly there."

Once again, I by another dying Christian stood,
A son of Samuel Everiett, Junior.
He had oft, with me conversed
About the family he was soon to leave,
When the hour for him to bid the world adieu
    was near.
He said, "Let me rise and pray."
But when his strength would not allow him
His bed to leave,

He raised a little, rested on one arm,
While he prayed for all.
A little later still, brother, wife, and children all,
Were seated round, when he said,
"I leave you all with God, for I am going home."
And calm and peaceful as a smiling babe
Within its mother's arms, he went to rest.
We cannot tell how soon our mortal life shall
 end:
So let us keep our lamps all trimmed:
For life hath thousand strings, which soon may
 break.

CHAPTER XXVII.—A SLEIGH-RIDE. A WISH.

I one day saw four young persons,
Full of life and health, merry, young, and fair;
They a sleigh-ride took,
And started from my parents' door;
But in one short year,
Three of the four were dead!
Once a young lady said to me,
"I wish that I could have the headache
One half hour, so I might know how it seems."
But ah! when a bride she stood,
The hectic flush, was on her cheek,
And in one year, consumption laid her low beneath the sod!
Her little Mary, which she left,
By the same destroyer fell!
Oh! let me tell, there is nothing firm—but heaven;
And there are consolations sweet, and joys divine,
Which we may taste on earth;
But there we shall know as we are known,
Our immortal powers made strong.

CHAPTER XXVIII.—CHRISTIAN CONVERSE, EXPERIENCE.

Now dear Christian friend, please let me tell you
How the Lord hath dealt with me:
I sought his face and asked
That he would all his grace bestow.
At church I rose and told what I sought.
And was about to take my seat,
Then quick as though , I had been struck –
I felt the power: I stood erect and said,
"I have got the blessing now."
And some good counsels I received that hour,
From friends who said, "Hold fast by faith,
Your heavenly Father's saving power, through
  Jesus' name confess;
And he will bless you, more and greater still."
So very strong was faith within my soul,
I said, I will, I do believe.
When two weeks had passed away,
In a prayer-meeting all were bowed in prayer.
God, saw fit to send the Holy Ghost,
With the Holy Spirit's power to fill the room.
Like to the ancient Pentecost.
One was there bent o'er with age, who said,

As long as I have lived,
I never saw what I have seen to-night."
The Holy Ghost was there with power divine;
To him be all the praise,
Till time with endless ages blend.
I had given soul and body to the Lord,
And Christ his Father, did reveal—
With power he shook this house of clay.
*I in an instant saw, that God the Father
Was the Holy, Holy, Holy One.
God in Christ his boundless love revealed,
And mercy, oh! how free.
Through my being these words were spoke with power:
"They will not come to me that they may have life."
Salvation, oh! how free and full.
The Holy Spirit filled my being—
A coal from off God's altar, had fallen on my soul,
And the weight of glory overpowered the mortal clay;
But Jesus and the angels were very near.
And Jesus, Jesus, Jesus, in my mouth and soul.
The river of the water of life,

---

*The writer's experience as to some of the great things of God, in the way of salvation, is not fully given in this work; yet the sentiments here expressed were deeply experimental.

How clear and sweet: I drank, and drank again.
Bliss we cannot speak: It will take eternity to tell.
Yes God is love, oh! blessed Christ,
The Lamb of God, a three in one.
The mystery is God's love, he calls himself my
   God—
He calls a worm his friend.
He taught me his almighty power,
O'ershadows those he loves;
And those who in him confide,
Shall rest secure beneath, the Almighty's shade
When our being fully purified, and we his temple
   are.
The immortal Jesus writes his name,
With the holy spirit's power, which the angels
   read.
A ransomed soul from every stain,
Through Jesus saved alone, this day I stand;
And on that rock so firm,
I build my hope of heaven.

> Borne on the wings of Jesus' name,
>   Prayer mounts above the storm:
> Moves him that moves creation's frame,
>   To listen and perform.

CHAPTER XXIX.—REMOVAL, SKETCHES BY THE WAY.

When about the age of twenty-one, my parents moved to the town of Rochester, Indiana, and remained there for more than two years. I have here found, a few scraps of writing, written during our stay in that place, which I will insert, as they in some measure show, how our feelings were exercised as time passed along.

JANUARY 20th, 1849.

I have this evening just returned from the church, where I heard an address from these words: "There remaineth therefore a rest, for the people of God." I have just looked upon the remains of a departed gentleman, who has left numerous relatives, and the church, to mourn his loss. Often have I heard that brother speak of the Canaan of rest. He has now passed Jordan a little in the rear—we shall soon pass the same; Jesus will be with, and cheer me through the gloom. It is time for me to renew my activity.— I have been too stupid. Oh thou blessed God, forgive, and for Jesus' sake, whilst thou givest me

a place among mortals, oh! never let me be guilty
of the blood of souls. Then mighty Savior if thou
seest fit to continue me here any longer, may I
feel the realities of eternity and act accordingly.
May I be perfectly holy, body and spirit. Give
me a spirit of gratitude; far more than I have
felt or exhibited. In a word, do thou take full
possession of every principle of my soul, body and
spirit. I am very vile, thou knowest I am dust.
—I am not worthy of the smallest favor from thee,
yet I look to Calvary. Oh! thou bleeding Lamb,
thou hast suffered for me. I am clay in thy
hands, mold me by thy power. I have often
grieved thee, yet thou hast been towards me a
God that forgives iniquity, plenteous in mercy
and abundant in goodness. Yes, I praise thee
for thy great love wherewith thou hast loved
such an unworthy one. I trust in thee. Amen.

JANUARY 21st, 1849.

Last Friday night I spent watching by the
death bed of a young lady, who had been taken
suddenly sick a few hours before. She had been
vain and thoughtless, and gave no evidence of a
change of heart. Sometime ago she was a member of my class at Sabbath-school. Several times
I saw her weep, yet she lived among those who
feared not God. She chose the vanities of earth,
rather than to suffer afflictions with the people of

God. Soon as she was taken, her speech became inarticulate—no time to prepare for death. Oh! shocking thus to go.

A very profane man died a few yards from us yesterday! He was irrational from the first attack of disease. He died—no hope. What a word; and can it be, eternity without hope? Time is but a moment, a part of eternity, a vapor soon past, yet dying mortals sleep on the edge of this precipice—this whirlpool, gulf or chasm. Oh! how can sinners sleep amid such scenes? The Holy Spirit alone can rouse the carnally secure sinners. "Ye will not come to me that ye may have life," says Jesus. They slight and grieve his dying, bleeding love; they slight joys immortal, crowns unfading. How unwise the baubles of earth, preferred to heaven. The serpent creeps where flowers are seen.—The poor stupefied victim of his malice, is lured on to ruin, by his devices, and by the charms and viles of a wicked world, and the false insinuations of satan, and a wicked or deceitful heart. Man presumes to sin, till justice takes his case in hand, and mercy retires. Last Friday night I closed the eyes of poor M. Her disease is considered by many very contagious. Many say that she and others have died with the cold plague here of late. I have been much exposed in turning over the body of poor M., as the last breath came directly in my face.

The ninty-first Psalm contains great promises. I am safe under the control of Almighty Love. I am in the hands of Jesus. He will take care of this frail tenement. I am safe in his power. He knows what is best and when to call his child home: his will be done. If he should call very soon, he will save me for his holy name's sake. I shall have passed through this dark valley, and emerged into that glory, of which I have had an antepast here on earth. Yes, a blessed foretaste —a home in heaven. Triumphant thought, bliss immortal. Adieu, vain world.

CHAPTER XXX.—MY ELDEST BROTHER.

In the year 1859, my parents changed their residence from Rochester, to Goshen, Indiana, and while there my eldest brother, after one short week of affliction, was called from earth to heaven. Oh! how much I loved him, when a fair sweet child, and a lovely youth.—But now adieu, we will soon meet again. The cares of earth will never fall on thee. Thou art at rest, adieu, dear brother, adieu. The funeral sermon of my brother, R. B. Abbott, was preached by the Rev. Vannuys, pastor of the Presbyterian Church, at that place. In the sermon which he delivered, he spoke of my brother, as a young man of great modesty and excellence.

Sleep, brother, sweetly rest, as Lazarus of old;
But when the Arch Angel's trump shall sound,
May I behold thee, lovely one,
With heavenly glories crowned,
And with the throng innumerable,
Traverse the happy land.

CHAPTER XXXI.—PROVIDENCES, AFFLICTIONS, A SACRED CHARGE.

In the fall of 1851, I was married to an honest, sincere Christian, Samuel Murray, who had long been a citizen of Goshen, Indiana, faithful in the church, abundant in charity, always helpful in church enterprise and all good. Our Bible was daily read and we bowed in deep sincerity before our Father's throne, feeling that God was our Savior and Redeemer continually. But the clouds of affliction commenced to lower around us, and we were made to feel the uncertainty of all earthly things.

My companion, about five weeks after our marriage, was seized with a severe lung fever, and brought down as it were, to the verge of the grave. After a partial recovery, he took a relapse of the same; and when to all human appearance, his eyes were closed in death, and all around said he is gone, I gave him a few drops of balsam, then his eye-lids moved, he revived, and spoke. His complaint assumed at this time a typhoid form. The windows of the room were shaded, and the utmost quiet preserved: Our heavenly Father, granted a helping hand and our afflicted companion was spared fourteen years. But his constitution, received a shock, from which he never fully recovered. To my parents is due many thanks for their kindness, during that heavy affliction. After this we lived in or near Goshen, Indiana, about eight years, and God gave into our charge, three little immortal ones.

The first a little angel spirit lent,
We called Mary;
And while our minister laid his hand upon her head,
He prayed that like ancient Mary,
She might sit at Jesus' feet.
The next, our William: a feeble tender child,
We gave in *covenant to God.
And then our Martha fair, we to God's altar brought;
The minister prayed that our babe might serve her God,

---

*The writer of this little volume was given in infancy to God, according to the custom of various churches and her three children were also covenanted under the same form; yet in after years Mrs. Murray felt convinced that according to the teaching of the New Testament she had a part to act, and in the spring season of 1879 went into the water near Goshen, Indiana, kneeled, and was baptized by pouring.

As a Martha did of olden time.
And soon we left for other land.
And took our lovely babes.
But ere we left, my father died!

CHAPTER XXXII.—DEAR FATHER.

Poor man, his was afflictions many;
He managed well, and toiled,
But losses came—loss top of loss, and sickness too.
But father dear, you are rich in heaven;
And we will meet you there.
The last words you to your daughter said on
    earth, were these:
"If we would with the pure and holy live in
    heaven,
We must be pure and holy here on earth."
And thus dear father, may I meet with thee in
    heaven,
And robed in angels' dress so free
Adore our King.
In Jesus' sweet embrace,
May thy dear spirit rest.
Your toils are o'er,
And heavenly glories now are thine,
With full fruition blest;
And near the great white throne.

CHAPTER XXXIII.—A SISTER ON CALAFORNIA SHORES.

And here I stop and think of one,
A sister very dear,
With whom I walked and talked;
Who went before my father died,
To Calafornia shores.
She was married at our parents' home,
And shortly started for the distant land.
Her companion, H. M. Porter, and herself,
Are numbered with the church militant on earth;
And may they when done with time,
With the church triumphant, in heaven rejoice;
And may their children three,
So many jewels shine in heaven.
And if that dear sister's face,
No more on earth I see,
May we clasp glad hands, with all dear friends,
When time with us is o'er;
And then with full immortal powers,
We will sing sweet strains of love.

PART SECOND.

---o---

CHAPTER I.—ON THE CARS. ON THE BOAT.

On the first day of April, 1860, my companion, with his little family, started on the cars for Kansas; and as we passed along, Lake Michigan seemed to lay high and boundless, while the zenith dipped its wings. And we were reminded of the boundlessness of space, and also of eternity without bounds. Here we might stop and philosophize, but we look back and think of friends, whom we had left in Goshen. Little did we know how long the separation might be,—and that some of us never would meet again on earth; but the cars rolled on till we stopped at Perue, Illinois. There was not at that day the same facilities for travel which our nation at present enjoys, therefore we took passage in a steam-boat, bound for St. Louis; and down the flowing, rolling tide our vessel urged its way. A few days passed, then we landed at St. Louis, changed boats, and started up the crooked Missouri River, bound for Kansas

City. The water of the river was muddy, and I saw dead cattle in the water along the banks. I remarked to a lady standing by, "I hate to see such water drank." But a man who was quaffing the same said, "Excellent water, madam, excellent water." The first day on that boat, a lady said to me, "you ask the proprietor of this boat, for a key to your berth room, and lock your door inside at night, for last night a man while sleeping in his room had his pocket cut open with a knife, and $500 taken from him." This was advice which persons in similar circumstances, would do well to remember.

CHAPTER II.—A GREAT PET. A BLACK COOK.

My little Martha, three months old, was a great pet with ladies, who said, "What a sweet babe Mattie is! what do you do with her? she never cries." But there was an old black cook who said to me, "Bless your life, mistress, I have sixteen children some-where in this wide world—they were all sold, and I can't tell where one can be found!" then she covered her face and wept. Surely separation of families, was a terrible feature of bondage. We may well be thankful for freedom and peace. May God save our country from every surrounding danger.

CHAPTER III.—AN EXPLOSION.

When we first started on this boat, there was much time spent in the large room of the boat playing cards; but one day our boat stopped and numbers came on board; and with the rest, a minister and his family. The minister's lady said, "The boiler of the boat they had left, burst, and soon as the explosion occurred, such swearing she never heard before!" The men employed on board said, "They knew something would go wrong, for there were so many white horses and preachers on the boat." But the lady said, "It was wonderful, that not anyone was harmed, for the boiler had burst similar to one that had exploded on the Ohio River, and killed many persons." In the first consideration of the case, we see superstition and sin, and in the second, the protection of the Almighty; and on a much higher scale of intellectuality do those stand, who fear and reverence God. The minister who had just come on board our boat, delivered us a sermon that evening; and we had no more card playing, but every evening was occupied in part with delightful singing. I had a bad cough during our journey, Mr. Murray and some of our little charge was not well, but a filial fear and trust in Providence, stayed our soul on God. Our boat at last landed at Kansas City, and we were taken in an omnibus to a hotel for the night.

CHAPTER IV.—DARK STAIRS.

A Methodist family, with whom we formed acquaintance on the boat, was with us. We were taken up several flights of stairs, to a square hall, and turning near the stairs found ourselves occupying a long bed-room, in the hotel. About the hour of retiring, one man entered another bed-room joining ours. There was only a thin partition between the rooms. Soon a man came into the hall, and locked everyone into their rooms. After all were sleeping, I still sat near a dim light sewing. Soon I heard the steps of two men come up the stairs. I heard them unlock the room where one man slept—then I heard deep groans, fainter and fainter, till all was still. Then I heard men pass our door with heavy steps, and down the stairs a load they took. In the Word of Truth we read, "The dark corners of the earth are full of cruelty." Before the darkness had come on that night, when a lady in our room and I were conversing of our prospects, I glanced around and saw two men under dark stairs, watching all we said. I could distinctly see their heads near each other, and their eyes shining in the dusk. Perhaps some reflection from other apartments, made them more visible. I used caution and calmness at the moment, and said, "our means in payments was to come." Now stranger, traveler, beware! for satan's servants walk this earth; and in proverbs we read, "The love of money is the root of all evil." And while you beware of men, ask God to save you from all sin; for often satan and his servants set gins, or snares, to trap the thoughtless, unprotected soul, and draw the wayward, wandering one farther and farther, down the steps of death.

CHAPTER V.—IN KANSAS.

When the following day arrived, a man who had brought a wagon load down to the boat, and would return fifty miles out into Kansas, said he would take us out to Mineola. And as we passed along o'er pleasant lands, we saw one section all fenced in with rock, in one enclosure. Mineola was in a beautiful country, but the land was a higher price than we wished to give. After a stay in that place of two weeks, Mr. Murray came into the dwelling where we had made our stay, saying, "In one hour and a half, we will leave for Emporia; as I have now an opportunity for conveyance." Mr. Murray had bought some things, and placed fruit trees in the ground, which were left, and never recovered. He thought he would secure those things, but failed. During our stay at Emporia we heard the gospel preached. But soon Mr. Murray picked up a paper that was blown across the street, in which the Cottonwood Valley was described. The next day he set out on foot and alone; he went fifty miles, located his land, bought a wagon and yoke of oxen, and returned. Soon his family were seated in a wagon drawn by oxen. To us this was a novelty never experienced before. But in all circumstances for one, I know, God was not forgotten. A man came back with Mr. Murray from the Cottonwood valley, where our land was located, and of whom Mr. Murray had bought the wagon--he came under pretense of business. His designs proved to be, to take every advantage of Mr. Murray, that satan could help a wicked man to devise. (Satan sometimes transforms himself into an angel of of light, to human appearance, and the worst side is not seen, till the false charm is broken.) That man got much help and money from Mr. Murray, for which there was no remuneration. We afterwards found he had sought the frontiers of Kansas, to avoid justice.

When we arrived on the Cottonwood valley, at first we did not stop on our own land, and the many trials we met the first few months, I shall not here numerate but pass them over.

CHAPTER VI.—THE FIRST INDIANS.

The first indians we ever saw.
Soon stood before the door,
With wild and savage mien;
And without any dress but just one piece,
And that was small.
Their guns and hatchets in hand,
They silent stood, and looked at us.
We thought we must not let them know we were
    afraid.
Soon they asked for bread and milk,
Then went away.
One was called Big Indian Jim,
And he had bragged how many white men's
    scalps
He had cut off from their heads.
I tell you, after they were gone,
I did not feel much strength.
Our health was delicate,
Perhaps that did our nerves effect.

CHAPTER VII.—CABIN HOME.

And when we would not longer stay from home.
We found our-selves in a new, hued log-house.
Our floor was not of plank, but just of earth.
Our window had no sash or glass,
And we had just an open door;
But we were greatly pleased,
To be once more at home,
And our little jewels free from evil influence.
We could gather our babes around
Our Bible read, and bow in prayer.
'Tis true, we were far from the pleasant home,
We once possessed, near Indiana's shores,
Where roses bloomed, and cherries ripened in the
    spring—
Where apples, pears, currents and other fruits
    were found.
Yet we could sound the praise of God,
On the extended plain,
Or by the ripening stream or skirting groves;
Or we alone could bow in pleasing groves,
And while we looked, far in the ether blue above,
Our faith took hold on God.
Wild plums were in abundance found.

And grapes along the streams.—
Birds sang in the groves,
Upon the hills the Indians often stood,
And we saw them walk near groves
And banks along the streams;
But we had learned to put our taust in God,
And feel that all was right.

CHAPTER VIII.—TWO SQUAWS.

One day on the prarie we looked
And saw indians start on an indian trail,
With spears and hatchets glistening in the sun.
For more than two miles
They stretched their numbers along the plain.
And still they came.
I stood with babe in arms within our yard.
Then I heard whoops and yells.
Indians passed our door, two squaws came in.
One was black. the other light enough to have
 been
A white woman just tanned.
She was troublesome and impudent.
They begged, then ransacked round the house.
The whitest squaw said, "Money in that trunk."
Then went to raise the lid.
Which I had left unlocked.
I told her, "Let that trunk alone.
If you don't, white man will take care of you."
She turned, looked at me, and said,
"No smokey man is here."
I told her, "There are two white men close by.

They will take care of you.
Let that alone."
They did not meddle more, but soon went away.

CHAPTER IX.—WE COUNTED SEVENTY-FIVE, AND STILL THEY CAME.

Once we looked toward hills, and saw Indians coming down. We counted seventy-five, and in numbers more they came, straight toward our house. All but one were Indian warriors; some were very dark, others much lighter, and features more regular. The squaw came first to the door. When she saw my fair babe, with flaxen hair, she raised both hands in wonder, and uttered exclamations in Indian dialect. Then the Indians of lightest caste walked up and spake in angry tones. I thought to my babe, they meant some harm; and if they had taken it by its heels, and dashed it on the wall it would have been just what I thought they said. But the squaw ran backwards the distance of several yards from their reach. The Indians were armed with everything white man or Indian would ever carry for warfare, revolvers, guns, long spears, hatchets, knives and Indian arrows, they displayed. But as if by some

---

Erratum.—The date on page 61, first line, should read, in the fall of the year 1849.

power beyond my own, I feared them not; I met the whitest ones at the door, as they came first. They shook my hand, gave their Indian salute, then asked for water. I gave them what was there, then they told me, "You go and get some more." I said, "No you go yourselves." I laughed, and showed them that I feared them not. Just then Mr. Murray came; He walked through the crowd that was around the door, and took his seat in the center of our room. He assumed a downward look, and would not speak to them. They tried to shake his hand, but he would show no sign of friedship. I gave them seats that were in the room. Six of them sat down and smoked, then said to me, "How many miles to the Arkansas River." I counted on my fingures, to show them the many miles away, then they motioned the way and said, "We go." Then all but one of those wild beings left our house and yard. But the remaining one stepped in the house, and looked round; he saw a satin vest and when he had surveyed it over, and saw it was old, he said, "No good." Then Mr. Murray said, "A mean Indian, very mean." But I said, "Hush, he is near the door." Then Mr. Murray said, "They might shake your hand, and that very moment, take your life." But I was carried above all, in perfect peace, by that Almighty Power that sways the rolling orbs, and gave the earth her frame.

CHAPTER X.—IN IOWA, MUCH LOSS, RETURN, BUFFALOES.

It was now in the fall of the year of 1860. The The settlers in Kansas had been too poor generally, to buy wheat for seed. They had depended for sustenance on raising corn, and all had failed, in consequence of a drouth that set in early in the season. A family left Kansas and went to Iowa: we went in company with them, and spent the winter in a house without a window. We had a very large fireplace and plenty of wood, and we had peace, trust and hope in God. And they of whom the world has not been worthy; and far better than we, have lived in dens and caves of the earth.

While at this place, Mr. Murray got the remainder of the money due, from the sale of our home in Indiana, sent to him; and on the first day of April, 1861, we started back to Kansas. When we came near St. Joe, we saw men running toward the town with guns in hand, and when we entered the town on business, we saw soldiers marching the streets with swords in hand, and wearing red shirts. The money Mr. Murray had, was nearly all on Missouri banks. The war had commenced, the banks had broke, and he could only get ten cents on each dollar, accordingly for at least $800, he only got $80. But Christ our Lord, the Lord of heaven and earth, had not where to lay his head. Mr. Murray had already secured 160 acres of land, and thither we proceeded. When there arrived, we found the valley had been covered with buffaloes. Hunters had found plenty of employment, for many heads and horns, lay on the prairie round, and our rough cabin door was taken down, and on it a buffalo had been dressed, and the head and horns lay in the middle of the room. We straightened things round, made them neat as we could, and again were at home.

Our time was employed with domestic affairs. Mr. Murray was busy planting his grounds, and cultivating the same; but visits from the Indians were frequent. About this time Mr. Murray wrote to his brother living east of us, that "our nearest neighbors on the west were at the Rockey Mountains." And surely if there were any white persons near the mountains, we were not there and it was two years ere we saw but just one white women; and she was no company for us: her husband was very wicked—he reverenced not God, and had very little regard for any one, his own family not excepted.

CHAPTER XI.—AFFLICTIONS.

The fall of 1861, afflictions came thickly around us, my little son had the chills and fever, and we had no medicine to give, till he could not stand alone; and my little Martha lost the power to sit alone. My dear Mary suddenly became very sick with congestion of the brain, and a very dangerous fever. I wet my daughter's head with camphor which we had in the house, and when the natural color partly returned to her face, I walked my yard in agitation; Then to my family I said, "Keep very still, while I run to a neighbor." I passed very rapidly a mile and a half, and through the providence of God, obtained the remedy necessary. I quickly returned, found my daughter in the quiet darkened room upon her bed, but irrational. The prescriptions were such as I had never administered before but through the blessing of Divine Providence, the fever abated as soon as the medicine took effect; yet I had to handle her like an infant for more then a week. we employed a man to go to the falls, twenty-five miles, and get medicine that broke the chills and fever on my other children. I had the chills also but never gave up for one hour to take my bed but continued every effort in my power for the comfort of my afflicted children. God brought us through those trials, and for six years afterward we had no severe afflictions of body, with the exception of Mr. Murray's poor health.

CHAPTER XII.—A DARK CLOUD, AN ADVENTURE.

Without the aid of machinery Mr. Murray with what assistance I could give him, succeeded in putting up for the winter following, two good stacks of hay. His wheat also made two nice stacks and a small one. The wheat was stacked across the river from our dwelling. Mr. Murray went to the wheat stacks and with a flail threshed out wheat sufficient for a grist then he cleaned and put it into sacks and left it uncovered in a rail pen. He had taken some pieces of carpet to the place and they was left on the side of the pen. Mr. Murray came home feeling very bad and laid down on a lounge. Soon a dark cloud lay along the horizon, thunders began to roll and the vivid lightnings to flash through the darkness that had suddenly settled around. Mr. Murray said, "Oh that threshed wheat will all be spoiled." Then I started out the door and in a short distance I ran in the darkness against an obstruction in our path. then I turned, went into the house and got a cane to feel my way. I told husband, "Never fear, I will fix all right about that wheat." The lightning very often showed the path—with my cane I journey on. I waded across the Cottonwood, then went across a prairie to a little creek skirted with timber. Here the wolves howled so near to me, that it seemed as though I could almost reach them with my hand: they seemed back of me, and on both sides, but as I walked onward I constantly whirled my cane around me, and thought perhaps I might hit one of those musicians. I again entered prairie, and the howling stopped. The lightning showed my pathway, and I soon arrived where the wheat was left, entered the enclosure and covered the wheat with carpet and straw. I had noticed two rails on one side of the enclsure, the lightning had revealed this to be on the side towards our home. I was about to direct my steps accordingly, when a flash of lightning revealed some object more frightful to me than even the wolves: it seemed to be a dark visage like some human being. I stood still and in another moment the lightning made visible the form of a black animal that stood confronting me, which I tried to lead for her company, but she refused to accompany me. Then I returned walking in the direction from whence I had come. I think the wolves were a little fearful; for I gained my home in peace. And there is a moral which may be drawn from my fright at the time mentioned. Sometimes things that seem to us evils, are only in disguise.

CHAPTER XIII.—A PRAIRIE FIRE, AND LOSS.

One day I saw smoke on high prairie above or back of hills. Mr. Murray lay sick on the bed. I told him, "Prairie fire is coming." He said, "It is not near." But soon I saw the fire roll along the hillsides; then I said, "Samuel come quick and help pull our wagon out from between those hay stacks, or it will be burnt up." We drew the wagon into the door-yard, and then the fire was very near, and as with a hurricane of wind, the flames, sut and smoke, were swept around. We got water and threw on things combustible near our dwelling, that we might save it from being consumed; but the hay stacks were soon in flames, and all around was like a sea of fire. It was surprising how the wind carried the fire—the waters of the Cottonwood stopped it not. The fire was carried in the air, and soon two large stacks of our wheat were consumed in the flames. But not a sparrow falleth to the ground without our heavenly Father's knowledge.

God moves in a mysterious way,
His wonders to perform.

> He plants his footsteps in the sea.
> And rides upon the storm.

In the midst of every trial or disappointment there was an Almighty Arm on which we felt to rest secure. And our soul enjoyed perfect peace, though our situation did not seem enviable, yet the God that feedeth the ravens cared for us, and we could trust in him, and realize sweet consolation and security, beneath the Almighty's shade.

CHAPTER XIV.—A POOR INDIAN.

The prairie range for stock was all burnt over, and our hay consumed by fire. But our cattle lived on browse about the streams. The Caw Indians often came and asked for bread, and when they received it, they would go and bring a larger crowd and were rather annoying. I was told, "You must not give them anything for they will make more trouble." Then I did wrong, for a poor Indian came to the door and said, "Give me *aid bread." I told him, we have nothing but what my pappooses need, and when he turned away, he coughed so hard, if I could have called him back, I would have given him bread. But he was soon carried by his pony from my sight. I never have since then, turned the afflicted poor away from my door unfed. Our heavenly Father accepts the kind acts done in charity to our fellow mortals, as done unto himself.

---

*The year of 1860, the crops failed in Kansas, and those who remained in the country the following season, and were destitute received aid from the States. In reference to this the Indian spoke of aid bread.

CHAPTER XV.—DEGREDATION.

By request, I will still relate more stories. It was a time of scarcity with the new settlers, and out along our fence, a large stray hog with poverty had died. Some Indians came and said, "Some hogy meet out there; give to Indian some." We said, yes. Then they went and cut the hams and shoulders out, then brought the kidneys in, and roasted them on coals, and laughed and talked, as though they had a fortune found. I think they were not as bad as cannibals, yet in them we see a state of degredation, by us abhored. But are our souls refined and free from all impurity? and do we feast on heavenly things, or are our souls with husks sufficed?

CHAPTER XVI.—A FLOOR OF ROCK.

I said to Mr. Murray, "Ground floor spoils our clothes. If you can't get plank, please get flat rock." Then we had a floor of rock, and on a carpet we did not walk. Yet we could contemplate the golden streets, and the paved walks of the New Jerusalem, and feel the heavenly breezes, wafted from the celestial shores, and sweetly sink into the will of God. Yet while we in this tabernacle of clay reside, temptations and trials may often be our lot and we may fail, through ignorance or weakness, from the perfect path of wisdom, yet the principle of soul for right, be firm for God and truth; and God looks deep within the soul, for he is omnipresent, evermore.

CHAPTER XVII.—AN INDIAN, A WHIP.

Now I will tell that which to you may seem sport. An Indian was at our home one day, and very troublesome. The Indian was in the dooryard. Mr. Murray wished to be at work, but was by the Indian detained. Then Mr. Murray drew his large ox whip, and I stepped between the two, fearful that the Indian would be angry and revengeful. Mr. Murray cracked the whip above the Indian's head, and said, "Clear out, you Indian." The Indian jumped away, then laughed hard as he could laugh. The reason for his mirth I cannot define, unless it were the novelty of his escape; but this I know, with hasty steps he left our home, to find his dusky friends at camp.

CHAPTER XVIII.— SQUAWS. "GIVE ME THAT CUP."

More of Indian mirth I will tell: Two squaws came to our house. They had a pappoose strapped on a board; they wished molasses, which I gave them in cups. I watched the teaspoons they were using; soon I saw one was missing. I walked close by and down into a budget looked and saw it shine. I put my hand within the budget and the teaspoon took. When they were gone, my little Martha said, "Ma, the squaw that had a little pappoose, took away my pretty cup." I looked and saw it was gone, then ran—hard as I could—and when I overtook the squaws, said, "Give me that cup." A squaw took the cup from under her belted blanket, got a little more molasses with her finger from the cup, then I took it; and when I had turned homeward, they laughed as though they had been glad; and in a very merry mood they were.

CHAPTER XIX.—THE INDIAN LULLABY.

I will relate what some child might please to read;
For children oft of others like to hear.
Caw Indians once were seated in our room.
One had long braided hair,
Hanging back with beads upon the ends.
My little Martha walked round.
Took hold of the beads,
And at them looked.
The Indian whirled, and caught her in his arms.
He dandled hushed and sung.
But she the louder screamed.
I said, "Give me that child;"
And then the music stopped.
But in the room an old dark squaw was seated.
And with her fingers she combed her straight
    black hair.
But if these are stories very small,   [Truth.
Dear child please look in God's holy Book of
And there you may read of the lovely Jesus;
The babe of Bethlehem.
Whom wicked Herod sought to slay.
Now if you wish to read that
Which may wisdom give,
Then study close the life of that Holy Child,
The Son of God, the babe of Bethlehem.

CHAPTER XX.—STRATAGEM, THE WICKED, THEY WANTED WHISKY.

We had a visit one day from a number of Indians who were partially intoxicated. They said, "Give us whisky." They carried long spears in their hands, and looked dangerous. I told them they were "mistaken in the place; for we never kept any whisky at our house." They said, they "heard there was some in the country, and were going to have it."

They started for the house of a Mr. H. There they found a barrel that contained whisky, and started to carry it off. Then Mr. H. said to his son, "Throw the yard fence down quick, so those white men can rush in fast, and take these Indians." Then they dropped the barrel and ran off. Mr. H. had only used a stratagem, and the Indians had shown cowardlyness.

The wisest, and most commendable deed would have been, to have made an opening in the barrel, and let the whisky run out on the ground.

Mr. H. had tried, like the wolf in a fable, to clothe himself in sheep's clothing, or to hide the worst side of his wicked doings.

His wife had terrible spasoms: perhaps one

cause might have been, the trial of having such a wicked companion.

They lived for a time a mile and a half from us. They were then the nearest white settlers; and when he had got all the money and work of Mr. Murray he could get, then I heard him swear, he would kill his own family.

I saw him take his coat off, and tell his old father, with oaths on his tongue; he would whip him, if he said one word on political questions.

I heard him tell a Mr. Miller, that he "killed a man in the state of Virginia, and ran away from justice, to the state of Missouri." And we were creditably informed, he had been run off from Missouri for misdemeanors. I heard him express his disregard for law, and realized that we had more of an introduction, to the way of the wicked, than was desirable. The way of peace they have not known. Their road is crooked, and leads to death. And I would with the poet say,

>Oh, dismal state of dark despair,
> To see my God remove,
>And fix my doleful station, where
> I must not taste His Love.

CHPTER XXI.—CHASING WOLVES.

Soon other settlers came to the country; our county was organized, and the town of Marion Center was commenced. In a short time after our first settling in the Cottonwood Valley, we commenced a little fun, which I will here relate.

Mr. Murray never owned a gun, and there were plenty of wolves in our vicinity. Some of different kinds; the smaller ones we did not fear.

One morning when we were all seated at breakfast, we heard a disturbance with the fowls in the yard, and heard them fly up on some new rails near the house. We suspected what was up and went quickly to the door. There stood Mr. Wolf, on his hind feet, his fore paws on the rails, and his mouth open for a grab at the fowls before him; just back of him stood a wolf watching the fun, and about three steps from him another one sitting down watching the first, and a little further on another sat. I picked up a clap-board that lay in the yard, and drew it in a threatening manner, spoke loudly, and walked toward them. They started off, but as soon as I was silent, they would sit down and look at me. Sometimes I stopped to look at them; then, with board in hand, rushed at them, at the same time making what noise I could. In this way I often ran them from our yard. But one day my two eldest children said: "We will never run wolves so far again; for we chased two wolves a quarter of a mile, and they sat down by a fence and would not go, but looked at us as though they meant harm." Then I said: "Sure you must not go so far to chase wolves again."

CHAPTER XXII.—MR. GRAY COAT.

But one morning, when seated at our accustomed refreshment, we heard noise from the fowls about six rods from the door.

I started with clap-board in hand; and, at the foot of a bank stood a large, heavy, gray animal, with heavy, black hair hanging thick and lengthy along the neck. I went right down the bank, toward Mr. Gray Coat. He would not turn around and run, but backed off side-ways, all the time looking me in the face. In this way I followed him, making what noise I could, looking at him, stepping toward him as he backed off, until he had passed over the little hill in the grove, and was nearing the creek bank. Then, in my haste to get out of the woods, I did not stop to count steps.

I have seen three other species of wolves, but never saw but the one that looked liked that. I have seen large, dark, heavy buffalo wolves; and the high, lank, timber wolves; and the smaller prairie wolves; but if that animal, which I chased from that bank of earth, near our home, and then across the wood, was a wolf there is no other species that I have seen, larger or more dangerous.

CHAPTER XXIII.—AN INVITATION. A SABBATH SCHOOL.

When busily employed with the occupations of domestic life, I heard a getleman conversing with Mr. Murray, in our yard.

After a short time Mr. Murray came into the house and said: "Mr. Phillip Frank has come ten miles—from Cedar Creek. There has been a missionary through that part of the country. The settlers along that stream, with the missionary's help have secured a Sabbath School library; but there is not any one to open or close the Sabbath School with prayer. Mr. Frank said he thought he would come and see if we would attend the Sabbath School; and if you go, you will have to ride on an ox wagon without any box, but only a plank.

I said: "I will go." Accordingly, the next Sabbath we went five miles to a Sabbath School, with our children three, and happy as though we had in a gilded carriage rode.

We found a goodly number of parents and children there for Sabbath School. A gentleman, by the name of Wrenfro, at whose house the Sabbath School was held, remarked: "My house is open for any religious services." And, after the hour of school was past Mr. Wrenfro and his hospitable lady said: "You must not return to your home until you have dined with us."

Their dwelling was a double log house of commodious dimensions, and well filled at our religious gathering. After such services, their table was amply supplied with excellent, nourishing food. Their hospitality seemed unbounded.

Buffalo meat, venison and fish were part of the viands.

At first their kindness almost overcame my self control, and my feelings would choke my utterance.

Soon after the organization of the school, an old gentleman, who stayed with his son on the Cottonwood Valley, and had acted in the capacity of a local preacher, visited our school, and preached two sermons; and we had one prayer meeting in which three prayers were offered which was very cheering and beneficial to me.

The last sermon that the elderly gentleman preached to the people of Cedar Creek, he told the people "either brother or sister Murray will read for you a sermon once in two weeks." The poor old preacher had to seek a home in other lands, for he met with unkindness from a wicked son. The last time I saw his face, he stood on a vehicle that was leaving the Valley. Looking back, he said: "Farewell! farewell! farewell Kansas!" But no doubt before this hour in which we write, he has been rejoicing with the ransomed in that blessed land, where fullness of peace and joy leaves no room for sorrow or woe.

CHAPTER XXIV.—READING SERMONS, SINGING, CELEBRATION.

Mr. Murray toiled, and labored far more than his health seemed to justify; he could not always attend our place of worship. Therefore I was chosen superintendant of the Sabbath-school; and Mr. Murray said, he "wished me to read sermons to the people," as they also desired; accordingly I acted in that capacity and never failed to be present at such appointments, till more than four years had passed away. Our friend, Mr. Philip Frank, taught the children to sing, and led the singing at our religious services. Our sermons were read from the Rev. Wesley's writings, or from Bishop Morris' sermons. Our heavenly Father granted His aid and blessings. I numbered and read our hymns which were sung with the spirit and understanding, and after sermons God helped me to speak whatever His Holy Spirit dictated on the occasion.

Once a Mr. S. at the time when persons were gathering for service, seemed inclined to sport; but a hymn was sung, commencing.

"Jesus let thy pitying eye,
Call back a wandering sheep.

False to thee, like Peter, I
Would fain like Peter weep."

And we sung again,

"O, Love Divine, how sweet Thou art."

Then a serious attention was expressed on every countenance, and God was there with His Divine blessing and heart-felt presence.

On a fourth of July occasion, parents and children for miles around, assembled in a grove near Cedar Creek. Mr. P. Frank, acted as president of the day, and displayed the spirit of an excellent citizen. He arranged the children, and trained them to sing for the celebration. He supplied the bountiful free repast, with some things which made a draft on his purse. Mr. F. made some remarks concerning our National Independance. We had singing, prayer and speeches from the children; singing, then intermission and free dinner. Friendship on all sides was unbounded. Then Mr. F. came to me and said, "We want you to give us an address." There were only a very few minutes for consideration. The seats were again resumed, utmost stillness prevailed, then the voice of song resounded through the grove. God quickened, enlightened and blessed. We spoke of the first introduction of Sabbath-schools, the happy influence of religion on youth, the consolations of the same in riper years; of intemperance as an evil, and the progress and practice of temperance as truly commendable; and of the beneficial results of Christianity in the civilizing of nations. Leaving ourselves in the hands of Almighty God: after singing and prayer, we left for our homes.

CHAPTER XXV.—NO MACHINERY. HEAVY TOIL.

After reaching our dwelling, the busy occupations of life were resumed; we had not the machinery which now helps to lighten toil. But Mr. Murray cut his wheat with a cradle, and I raked it into bunches with a garden rake, then Mr. Murray bound it in bundles, and I and the children shocked it up. When it was stacked, I pitched the bunches for him to stack, and morning and evening milked several cows. But a heavy pain in one arm and shoulder, attended with numbness, often prevented my rest at night. Yet, we tried to do all we could, for Mr. Murray had no other help. The flail, with which our grain was threshed, was formed by tying two sticks together, and leaving one to fly like a heavy lash, to strike the unthreshed grain. That sort of work Mr. Murray should not have done, as anything like dust was injurious to his lungs.

CHAPTER XXVI.--PRAIRIE FIRE. GOD'S HELP.

The grass on the prairie was growing more dry every day. The smoke of the prairie fires in the distance were numerous. There were indications of an approaching conflagration, and no protection for anything combustible. And only Indian trails through the grass north and west of us.

We were beginning to have some experience in these things, and found that by taking advantage of the wind we could whip out the fire with wet sacks and brush.

Smoke and fire appearing still more near, gave us cause for action. Mr. Murray said: "I will go and whip out prairie fire from a bend of the Cottonwood river across to another stream below."

Mr. Murray and our eldest daughter went to the scene of the fire, and were gone a long time.

Our youngest children were sleeping. Once I thought the fire was nearly out on the hills, but then it spread and was running in a solid line. The flames dispelling the darkness of night. I took a sack in a pail of water, and in haste went to the line of fire, and commenced to battle with the flames, by beating the burning sod with the

the wet sack. Thus I whipped out fire for fully one long mile. I saw that Mr. Murray was not near, and the wind had raised. I went to our home, and found Mr. Murray and my daughter.

I said: The fire is coming fast." He remarked. "I have whipped it all out."

The mistake was that the fire had caught back and spread, and was running in a long line, swept forward by the wind.

Mr. Murray started to meet the advancing conflagration. I accompanied him. We toiled rapidly to stay the impending evil, but a strong wind carried it swiftly forward. Then Mr. Murray said: "You go to the house and watch things there; perhaps I can do a little here.' I went and got two pails of water, and another sack, and went between the field fence and the fire and sat down in the grass. Then I prayed: "O! our Heavenly Father. Thou canst stop the consuming element. Thy hand is omnipotent. Thou canst say hither shalt thou come and no further."

The grass was very dry. The wind was high, and there was a long line of fire. The fire went out all along the line of hills north of our home. I know it was God who done that work; for the ravines and bottom land was full of dry grass, and nothing but the hand of Providence stayed those flames.

> The trusting child of God,
> Though like the Hebrew children tried,
> Shall conquer every foe.
> For lo, with them the fourth,
> The Son of God was seen.

CHAPTER XXVII.—WHAT WE HAD FOR FOOD.

I heard one say: "What did you have for food on the frontier of Kansas?"

I will tell you. Mr. Murray's health was poor. He never went on a buffalo hunt; and when he went to mill sometimes, he could get nothing but shorts. Our bread was often made of corn meal. Sometimes we had wild fruit, but very little meat. Sugar and molasses were scarce, at our home. Coffee and tea from stores did not visit us.

However, we made substitutes of rye and prairie tea. In the winter we scarcely ever had any milk, for our cows would go so far on the range, the milk would fail, for we would not get them always. We kept fowls which were much help, and through the spring and summer we had plenty of good milk and butter.

We called all persons our neighbors within ten miles from us. Sometimes they would send us buffalo meat, which is wholesome food; but when we had nothing except warm shorts biscuit, my children received them thankfully, and I felt as thankful as though we had dined on rich viands, at a king's table; and our songs were as cheery as the happy birds in the groves along the streams.

I did not wish our cows to fail in milk, and went three miles on foot to find them. One night they did not come home, but with the first sign of day, I carefully left my home, when all my family were asleep in slumbers of the twilight, and went about three miles on foot, got the cows, and returned about breakfast time. My family had just begun to think, "where's mother?" but the children were glad of nice milk, and this is a true saying:

> "Better is a dinner of herbs where love is,
> Than feasting and hatred therewith."

CHAPTER XXVIII. ELEVEN DAYS ABSENT. HE WENT TO MILL.

Mr. Murray had to go to Council Grove, forty-five miles or to Emporia, fifty miles from us, to get any milling done, and sometimes could not get it done, but had to exchange for whatever he could get. Once the mill at Emporia was broken, and was undergoing repairs. Mr. Murray was not well when he left home, and we felt anxious about him. He was gone eleven days, which was longer than usual. Our bread failed, and my children lived three days on boiled wheat. I did not dare to let my children know how much I feared something had went wrong, as to their father's health.

In all such journeys he camped by the road side, and seldom stopped at night at any dwelling. I went to our nearest neighbor's house and told them our fears and anxiety, and they kindly promised that if Mr. Murray did not come home that night, a man should start the next morning to find him. Then I went two miles to hunt the cows; and when returning, saw his wagon come in sight. The children were soon running to meet and welcome their father. We soon met, and were glad to find him well. He told us he had to go much farther than Emporia, and then had to wait some time to get anything. And we, like Paul, of whom we read in God's holy Book, have learned both how to abound and how to suffer need.

   Oh! may we, when this short life is done,
   An unbroken number make,
   So near the tree of life in heaven;
   That, in concert we may take the golden fruit,
   And of the living fountain drink;
   Which flows from the white throne.

CHAPTER XXIX.—IN ALL OUR WALKS AND LABORS HAPPY.

We had to cross the Cottonwood river to get any spring water. Sometimes a spring afforded water about a half mile from home, sometimes we had to go much farther; and when Mr. Murray would come in from work, I knew he would be thirsty. Therefore I always brought cool fresh water to the house for his benefit. I kept a Testament in my pocket, and read a chapter, as I walked in the pathway. I generally carried a small hymn book also, and if the country had been a desert, it seemed to blossom as the rose, and with gladness to break forth into singing.

Mr. Murray worked very hard, considering his state of health, and when he came in from labor, sometimes he would get down on some hard place to rest. Then I would place a pillow under his head. And I know that as long as he lived, he remembered with gratitude, the many little attentions he received.

I carried our wood from the time spring commenced, till winter arrived at the close of fall, in my arms from a grove near by. And in all our walks and labors, we were happy; and why should we not be? Paul and Silas sung the praises of God in prison, and their feet made fast in the stocks. But free as the birds in the groves, we could hold sweet communion with God. And our lovely children run to meet us in our pathway and we could sing:

> "Our pathway bright,
> With heavenly light,
> And innocence, and smiles;
> Though satan grudge,
> The vain might scorn,
> Yet Jesus blest His own."

CHAPTER XXX.—THROUGH A SNOW BANK AND GOT WOOD.

Mr. Murray could work in pleasant weather, but sure as there was a change of weather and snow, his lungs distressed him, and he was sick. It snowed very hard one night, and snow drifts were very deep. The down wood in the timber was all hid by the snow. No wood at the house, and Mr. Murray sick in bed.

I took our ax, and found my way through a snow drift, down a high bank to timbered land, cut limbs from trees, and carried them to the house for wood. By this means we were comfortable; and, after a few hours Mr. Murray's health returned.

There was about three years of frontier life that our nearest neighbors east of our dwelling were three miles off, and at that time we did not know of any settlers west of us. The place where Marion Center now stands, was in a north-west direction, and very few settlers were then near the place. But antelope and Indians ranged at large on the wide-spreading plains, or near the cooling streams.

CHAPTER XXXI. RED PAINT AND WAR SONGS.

One day, about this time, a large Indian came into our dwelling, seated himself, and proceeded to put much red paint on his face, and in his hair. Then he stood before our glass and surveyed his copper-colored and painted visage. Perhaps he thought he made an elegant appearance, for he soon commenced to dance and sing Indian war songs in his own dialect. Surely such sounds could never be music for any but a savage.

CHAPTER XXXII.—CEDAR CREEK SNOW STORM.

After cares of the week were over, and the holy Sabbath had shed a soft light on all nature round, I started on horseback for Cedar Creek, where parents, youths and little children met to sing songs of Zion, and consider the language of the revealed will of God, and to listen to the councils of His servants, who "though dead yet spoke."

We had left our little family with the peaceful halo of the sacred Sabbath around them, and as usual, our gathering together was truly beneficial. There had been rain, but when I went to return home, there was round snow falling. Mr. and Mrs. Wrenfro, at whose house we had met, went to see me on the horse. The wind was driving rather roughly, and they had wrapped me all around with a thick blanket, and put it over my head. After I started I found that if I uncovered my face the wind drove the snow in my eyes so that I could not see. I therefore kept the blanket sheltering my face from the driving storm. I guided my horse in one direction, and he tried to go in another course. Soon I saw I was lost. Then I gave the horse loose rein, and he took me the straight way for home.

The next day, while engaged in our duties of life, Mr. H., whom we have already mentioned, entered our dwelling. He was very full of laugh and said to me:

"You got lost yesterday, for I saw your horse's tracks. How glad I would have been, if you had got away off on some distant stream and had to stay all night. It would do me more good than anything else, if you would have had to stay out doors and lost, without any fire, and in that storm."

Then I said that if I had stayed all night in the storm, far from habitations, not knowing whither I had wandered, it would not have harmed me, for I had been doing my duty, and I would have been very happy. I know that I should have praised God for helping me to suffer so much for Christ's sake. His countenance changed to that of solidity. He said nothing more, but soon went to his own quarters.

> Our God can quell the hate of man,
> And bless with honor, strength and grace,
> His trusting little ones.

CHAPTER XXXIII.—FOUR SAVAGES.

Mr. Murray was absent from our dwelling. I and my children were employed with our accustomed duties, or entertainments. When four large dark looking savages, entered our dwelling. Those Indians were much darker than the Caws, and all the clothing they wore was just one small piece. They spoke no english, but seated themselves in our room and sharpened large knives, then they felt the edges with their fingers, to see if they were rightly prepared for use. They appeared very grum, and wild.

We were defenceless to human appearance, yet our trust was in Him that made the world, and holds by power Omnipotent the circling orbs, and in that power we were safe and free from harm.

CHAPTER XXXIV. MET THE CANNONS' ROAR.

War, within the bounds of our beloved Union, our lovely country, which has caused many happy homes, to be shrouded in mourning, was in progress. My youngest brother went to meet the canon's roar—the smoke and din of numerous battles, and to behold the horrors of war. His innocent face in childhood and youth, is pictured on the mind's eye of memory, in lines too vivid ever to be effaced. And when manhood had but recent marked him for its own, that brother of manly form, gentlemanly in deportment, standing high in intelligence, and on the very pinnacle of educational fame, to whom higher science had proved but pleasant pastime, esteemed and loved by all who knew him, left his widowed mother, whose anxiety was far reaching, and very extreme for his safety, and went to meet scenes of conflict.

He had been editor of a paper in Goshen, Indiana, when a mere youth, and now mother sent us the papers in which a number of his letters were printed, giving accounts concerning battles, in which he had been engaged. He also wrote to my daughter Mary, expressing kind sentiments, and much sympathy, for suffering, distressed fellow beings, with whom he met. And those who may still survive the ravages of war, and were in company I, 74th regiment of Indiana volunteers, would gladly testify, that his kindness, noble bearing and generous spirit, has not all been told.

Captain Everiett Abbott sustained a relation to the readers of a political paper for the period of five years.* And with reluctance he gave the parting hand to the brethren of the press. We here quote some of his farewell language.

"All the feelings of bitterness which have been engendered by political antagonism have been forgotten by me, and henceforth I shall only retain the memory of so much of my intercourse with them, as has been mutually pleasurable. Farewells at this time, when the country is calling for speedy action, should be briefly spoken. And so to readers and friends, one and all, good bye."

His influence for good morals and literature, was highly felt while in the army, by all with whom he was associated.

Only twenty-one years of age at the time when he left the printing office, in Goshen, yet his young life blood soon to be laid at Columbia's feet. Among some of the pure sentiments of his

---

*Wm. A. Bean is editor of the same paper at the present time.

youthful mind, we notice prose which we here insert as a memoria:

LIKE AN ANGEL.

"'Why, you would have me like an angel!' Said a young and beautiful girl, accompanying the expression with a toss of the head, and a light, but somewhat disdainful laugh. Perhaps the words were addressed to a maiden aunt, who may have been reproving her rather severely for some thoughtless coquetery. And why not be like an angel! Indeed there can be no harm in becoming so.

"Angels are said to be very beautiful, and which is far more to be desired, their natures correspond with their forms. They are gentle, compassionate, loving and sinless. These are not forbidden traits. Angels cherish no evil passions in their bosoms. They wreathe not their faces in smiles, while hatred and envy are corroding their hearts. They entice not with the eye to cast coldly away with the lip. In their beautiful home they meet not together to asperse the character of the absent. They rejoice not in injury to anyone. We are told that among them are seraphs and cherubs—beings of beauty, tenderness, and love, and though you have not their wings, your beautiful form will befit the virtues of which they are possessed.

"Do you never wish that you may sometime

really become an angel? If so, be as near as possible like one now. Be pure in thought, and gentle in spirit. Discipline your mind by good deeds for the high destiny. By this means you will surely become, if not a bright angel in heaven, at least what is next to it, a true woman on earth."

The lines we have here inserted, was written when the author was fifteen years of age. We pass by many other sentiments equally ennobling and refined and leave him on battle fields meeting a soldier's lot, beloved by the company who claimed him as their captain, to which position he had risen by merit. And we return for a season to those scenes that transpired around us.

CHAPTER XXXV.—DOLEFUL LAMENTATIONS.

Rumors frequently reached us of bands of Indians led by white men, making depredations in some parts of the country. The Caw Indians were loyal to our nation, and some other tribes seemed to wish them extinguished.

One day several Caws entered our dwelling; they were painted red, and said, they were "on the war path." They remained in the house a short time, begged a little, then took a westward trail.

The Indians west of us, used much effort to prevent the Caws from hunting buffaloes, driving the buffaloes farther back, and westward, and killing the Caws.

After a few days had elapsed, the Caws returned from their westward course, and camped half a mile from us. That night the doleful lamentations, and horid powwow, seemed as though it had issued from some dismal pit. When the morning sun was sheding forth its halo of light, Mr. Murray directed his morning walk to their camp. He made some inquiries, and the Indians told him, their enemies had shot one of their number, and killed him, and they were conveying him back to their burial ground. Perhaps they imagined there was some merit in the doleful sounds uttered by that entire party of Indians, at the first dawn of day that morning.

CHAPTER XXXVI. A JOURNEY, A POW-WOW, AND BURIAL.

We had made arrangements for a journey to Council Grove, near the Caw reserve, for the purpose of selling a load of wheat to buy clothing with the value of the same. Five in number we started after having secured a gentle cow to the back of the wagon, thus providing for the nourishment of our children as we journeyed.

We had to travel slowly. I carried with me a supply of good material for reading. After we had proceeded a few miles on our journey, we arrived at the dwelling of an acquaintance, where our Mary remained until our return. After traveling some miles further with our heavy loaded wagon, when about to ascend an elevation of land, we left our little son to drive the oxen (which he was accustomed to do), and walked back of the wagon. The oxen became unmanagable, and the child leaned hard on the fore-board, which came out. He was precipitated forward—the beard fell, and lay on his head. The oxen continued their course. One wheel of the wagon ran across one corner of the beard, marking it and sliding off; one wheel also grazed and bruised one hip. Mr. Murray picked him up: I said, "Oh! is he killed?" but he soon spoke, saying, "My head, Oh! my head." We carefully placed him on the grass, and found cool water, with which we bathed his bruises.

(Truly the future is vailed from our view and we know not what may be on the morrow.) But again we proceed on our way. When the hour to camp for the night arrived, we found ourselves near the Caw reserve land. Indians came round our camp fire, but said nothing, and soon left us. That night their powwow, exceeded all we had previously heard. They had something with which they made a ringing sound, and their doleful noises all in concert with the same. There were many Indian camps along the stream, on the bank of which we had stopped. The powwow, undescribable, would commence with one camp and take a perfect round. Then the sounds would start round again, from one camp to another.

When morning arrived, and displayed the autumnal dress of nature, we were reminded of an ever present Deity. And soon we were on our journey. When we had passed along some distance and in sight of high hills, a procession of Indians came from some timber, and crossed a strip of prairie, carrying a dead Indian, on a rude bier, formed with poles and strips of bark, and carried by four large Indians. The dead Indian was wrapped in his blanket and in the manner described, carried to the top of the highest hill visible. Our observations could extend no further, as to the proceedings of that occasion. But I have stood on the top of a high hill, not far from my home, and looked into a rude enclosure formed by a circle of rocks, and within that circle, beheld the bones of an Indian, also other bones, and I suppose they had killed his pony and dog, that they might bear him company, to the better hunting grounds.

We arrived at the place of our destination: Mr. Murray sold the wheat he had brought for market; we secured things necessary and moved homeward.

CHAPTER XXXVII.—TEXAS, AND MEXICAN TRAINS, A FARCE.

But ere the journey was over, we had witnessed the movements of Mexican and Sante Fee trains, of which if we had taken some note, we could better describe at this time. Council Grove was a trading point for Mexican trains—other trains conveyed provision from that point, to distant forts. The American government trains, with large government wagons, were drawn frequently from that point by cattle; but the Mexican trains had six span of ponies, attached to each large loaded wagon.

The Mexicans rode astride their ponies, and I think no other person could throw their long lash of whip with the same dexterity, and certainty of effect which they did, as they uttered their peculiar "twang and chee." A train was not composed of one wagon and its appendages, but of a number, and sometimes their line of procession was quite extensive. I have witnessed their movments at several different times. Once as we stopped to prepare an evening repast, and camp for the night, a Mexican Train stopped a little distance from us, kindled their camp fire, arranged their ponies for the night, and seated round in squads, partook of their food. Then some of them walked near and gazed at us. Their curiosity having subsided, they returned in a short time to their own camp. Then commenced a pretended battle. I suppose there were not less than sixty Mexicans in that company. They made much noise and brandished large bowie knives in the air; and motioned as though they would plunge their weapons, into the bodies of the ones with whom they were engaged. Their bright camp fire with the clear beams of a full moon shining round, made every movement very visible.

After their commotion had abated, and those boistrous ones had retired within their camp, I committed my family and myself anew into the care of Omnipotence; and after refreshing slumbers rose at an early hour to prosecute our journey.

There is much variety in the face of the country in the state of Kansas. Some parts by nature are more calculated for cultivation than others. The skirting groves, the rippling streams, the level bottom land prairies, or the gradual rolling plains, or more steep ascents, all show forth the works of God. But we are again at our dwelling on the Cottonwood valley, ready to resume our occupations there.

CHAPTER XXXVIII.--A PAIR OF MOCCASINS.

I taught each one of our children to read when they were quite young. Books took up much of their time and attention; especially our Mary, whose delight in learning was constant. The Caws would be very quiet when my children were studying their books.

There was a missionary a short time at the Grove. An Indian acted as interpreter; he often visited our dwelling, and spoke very good English. Once he brought his squaw with him, and said, "We are hungry." I prepared a table for their refreshment. After the meal was over, the Indian spoke a few words in his own dialect; then the squaw opened a budget, from which she drew a beautiful pair of moccasins, covered with flowers formed with beads. She made me a present of them. And in speaking of me to our neighbors afterwards, he called me his mother. The Indian just mentioned, called his name William Johnson. He was a chief. Once several Indians came with him to our home. When they commenced to beg, he ordered them to leave, and they obeyed. Then he told me, "They don't need anything."

Wm. Johnson said, "White men about the Grove, would steal horses, and say the Indians had done it." He said, "White men are just as bad as Indians."

We afterwards found, that a gang of horse thieves, had made their head quarters at the Grove. The law was put in force and their opperations checked. The Caws sold many furs and buffalo robes at Council Grove.

CHAPTER XXXIX.—"SISTER, PLEASE GIVE ME A CUP OF WATER."

When occupied with household duties, and sometimes singing the sacred hymns which we had learned in other days, we heard a sound of coming steps, and saw an Indian ride before the door. He said, "Sister, please give me a drink of water." He took the cup which I presented, quaffed the sparkling draught, returned the cup, saying, "Thank you, sister." Then he placed his hand on his heart, and said, "Indian good in here, are you good too?" When I the infirmation gave, he bowed and went away.

Thus we see a little of the refining influence, the sacred Gospel can bestow.

CHAPTER XL.—DRIED IN INDIAN STYLE.

After some time had elapsed, William Johnson again visited us. He said, "I am going on a Buffalo hunt, and have nothing for bread." Mr. Murray lent him a sack, and let him have twenty-five pounds of flour. The Indians and their chief, were gone on their hunt about two weeks. When they returned, Wm. Johnson brought us very sweet, nice looking, Buffalo meat. It had been cut in strips and braided like basket work, cured or dried in Indian style, and several feet square. My children and some other persons, partook of the meat with relish, but I was possessed of a little prejudice in the case.

CHAPTER XLI. HE CAME FOR PROTECTION.

One evening, as the sable curtain of night was closing round us and offering rest to the weary, an Indian presented himself at our door and desired to remain in our dwelling over night. I consulted Mr. Murray, then gave the permission and prepared a pallet on the floor; the Indian was soon stretched on it fast asleep. In the morning after rising from his rest, he asked for water, bathed freely, and partook of the morning meal which we offered.

We were informed afterwards, that the Indian had come to us for protection from his enemies.

CHAPTER XLII.—THEY HAD ASHES ON THEIR HEADS.

About an hour before the queen of day had closed her mission for those hours, several camps of Indians came in sight of our dwelling, and stopped for the night. Toward morning especially about the time a little sign of day appeared, many doleful sounds and lamentations, aross from their camps. The stillness of the night air allowed those sounds to reverberate along the groves, and streams.

After the refreshments of the morning hour were over, and the reading of the Inspired Volume, and family devotion led by our companion, Mr. Murray directed his steps toward the Indian camps; there he saw a squaw with ashes on her head and face, her tears had made their lines, and mingled with the same; and half a dozen youths and pappooses had ashes on their heads, and their faces streaked with the same. Mr. Murray inquired what was the cause of sorrow; they said, "One little chile die three days ago."

The government built houses for the Caws, and the houses were painted white, but most of the Caws chose to put their ponies in the houses, and stay out in their Indian tents themselves.

CHAPTER XLIII.—FOUR SAVAGES PULLED HIM FROM HIS HORSE.

Mr. Murray was always pleased, that we should serve God faithfully, and do his will, and when he was not too much exhausted, with the toils in the week, he attended his family to the place of worship, bearing a part of the same. And religion was the sacred bond that united our souls in unison to God.

After one of the services, which was closed with the benediction, a young man remarked: "I have come twenty-five miles to this meeting, and would go that far any day to such a meeting." The young man just mentioned, was herding cattle west of us soon after that, and four large savages were seen to pull him from his horse, scalp him and drag him off. His poor old mother never saw him again. Often I have seen her tears, and anguish heave her breast, while of this kind son she spoke.

CHAPTER XLIV.—A TRAIN ROBBED.

About this time, a neighbor, who lived three miles east of us, Mr. Brenot was employed to haul provisions to a fort. The Indians attacked his train, killed sixteen yoke of oxen, took possession of all the provisions, and a young mare which Mr. Brenot had with him for riding purposes. Mr. Brenot and his hired men, merely saved their lives, from the power of the savages by flight. For when deadly weapons, and savage purposes were brought into action, that was their only resort.

At that very time when Mr. B. was absent, a prairie fire swept away much of his property; thus he was subject to discouragment and loss.

CHAPTER XLV.—A STOLEN ANIMAL.

Mr. Murray had bought a mare and colt, and it seemed very necessary that we should have the service of the large animal; but soon they were missing. They were gone several months; but I felt perfectly assured, they would be restored. A neighbor entered our home, and after usual salutation, said, "The Kicapo Indians have sold your mare and colt for a sack of flour, a little south of here." He accompanied Mr. Murray, and when they returned, they brought the missing animals.

I had fully believed that God could and would restore them—we were His children—the necessity of our case seemed to demand their restoration.

CHAPTER XLVI. AN INDIAN FEAST.

Mr. Murray did not wish to keep a dog that had been given to him. A large Indian said, "Swap." The agreement was made, then the Indian took a wide long belt of leather, covered with flat pieces of brass, lapping one on to the other the whole length of it. These he fastened on the animals neck with brass fastenings so securely that he knew we could not release him. Then the Indian refused to comply with the conditions of the trade. The savage held his butcher knife in hand and though much we regretted the fate of the animal; he was treated according to heathen dictation.

The Indian made the dog open his mouth, into which he spit three times, said a few words in Indian language, looked the dog in the face, then threw tobacco in his mouth, and dragged the poor animal after him to his pony, then dragged him onward.

I suppose the Indians feasted on the animal; for once they begged a cat, and when we passed near the camp, they had it dressed for their food.

CHAPTER XLVII.—ANTELOPE AND TURKEYS.

I have seen antelope in gangs, of from fifteen to twenty-one: but Mr. Murray was no hunter, and never owned a gun. He said, "I have no time to hunt;" and he was constantly employed. He said, "I wish we had been married much before we were, and that I had always worked out in the open air, and not spent so much time in stifled air, in a shop. Sedentary employment is injurious, and farming is the most independant business."

One morning when seated at breakfast, a gang of turkeys came close round the house. Mr. Murray said we should not frighten them away. We kept quiet till they left; then Mr. Murray made a large rail trap, and said they would be back again. Toward evening they returned; soon they all were caught. Then another flock of wild turkeys came round, and they shared a similar fate. He also made another trap, of different dimension; and sometimes prairie fowls were caught.

Mr. Murray was very reserved in speech; but when he spoke, it was with meaning. Of his children he thought much; and when two of they were away from home, the Cottonwood stream was high, he thought they might be drowned, and his anxiety was extreme; but soon they came. And when his little son had just put on new clothes, the child thought he would have a ride; he took a horse to water, and when he did not return, we thought perhaps the Indians had stole our child. And while I looked along the streams and called his name, Mr. Murray hastened to a neighbor's house, and there found his boy. The children needed such a father to guard their steps from harm; to council and to lead, and save from youthful snares.

CHAPTER XLVIII.—SCALPS OF ENEMIES.

Indians of different tribes, would often come round. Some wore heavy bands of brass on their arms. Some had many holes cut in their ears, and rough rings inserted in the same; and from holes cut in their noses, rough rings hung. Sometimes they carried by our door, the scalps of enemies; and once my children said, "Oh, ma, those Indians that just passed our door, had white men's scalps; they were hanging from a pole, the hair was fine, and lighter color than the Indians' hair, and the hide which showed was white, and they may kill us." I strove to soothe their fears and trusted in God.

About this time Mr. Catlin moved into a cabin just one mile from us. We were glad to have a neighbor near as that, on the frontiers.

CHAPTER XLIX.—FLIGHT FROM SAVAGES.

About dusk one evening, Mr. Catlin rode up to our door and said, "The savage Indians out West, are coming right this way, and killing every hunter, and every one they meet, and driving off or killing stock. I and my wife are going to start in a short time in our wagon, to get away from those wild Indians; and if you will get over to our house very soon, you can ride with us in our wagon." Mr. Murray told me "Take the children and go; but I shall remain; and if I ever leave, I never will come back; but if I am left alone, I will keep out of the Indians' way."

I had just baked plenty of light loaves of bread. I placed several small loaves in a sack, and in another sack placed each one a change of clothes, tied them quickly together at the top, and placed them on a horse on which my children rode. We left Mr. Murray plenty of bread, milk and batter. We had very little time for parting words; our neighbors could not wait. Indians might overtake us, and our scalps would pay the forfeit.

We hurried on, and by our neighbor's yard

two wagons stood, with a family in each. They quickly took my children and our sacks into a wagon, and I on horse-back rode. Each wagon was supplied with those things which in their haste, they had gathered up for their necessities.

But as we eastward hurried, a wagon-tire came almost off. We stopped and wrapped the tire with rope, but our moments were very choice. Again, we hurried along. It was past the hour for children's rest; my little William went to sleep, and dreamed that he saw Indians after him; then he jumped and went like he had wings, out of the wagon over on the ground. The company wondered, that the child seemed unhurt.

After traveling twelve miles, we came to a good sized rock house. Families were all collected at that place from Cedar Creek; and from along on the Cottonwood. They had concluded in case of an attack, to make the rock house answer the purpose of a fort, and fight from that place if necessary. They also sent out men to watch the Indians, and find out what they were doing. They soon found that the Indians had changed their course, and went in another direction; and after a day and two nights' absence, we returned home, found all right there, and Mr. Murray glad of our society again. The children had forgot, to all appearance, the hours of fright and were glad to be at home. But soon we heard a little, of what the Indians had done.

CHAPTER L.—SAVAGE INDIANS, A RACE FOR LIFE.

Several of our neighbors, had been carelessly pursuing a westward course, looking at the face of the country, and pursuing wild game, when the Indians suddenly rushed near them, shot and killed one young man, and thought they had killed another. They shot and scalped him. He lay perfectly still on the ground, while they stuck spears into his feet, to see if he was dead. He was picked up by white people and afterwards recovered.

They shot an arrow into the shoulder of one man, where it remained for some time before it was extracted. The wound was inflicted when he was running from his foes. He succeeded in reaching the shelter of timber, and concealed himself along the banks of streams, till he arrived at his own settlement.

A boy was in the company. Those that survived, said, "They could not have been made to belive, any human being could have jumped as far as he did with every bound, while he fled from the Indians." I think he would never forget that race for life.

Mr. Smith had a ranch near the Sante Fee

road. At that place the Indians contented themselves, with driving off large fine horses. The man and his wife who kept the ranch, left very soon, fearing the Indians might return and take their lives.

CHAPTER LI.—ON A STORMY SEA. TESTIMONY.

And now, dear friend, in view of the dangers with which we were surrounded, let no one suppose that God forgets for one moment, his lowliest child that trusts in Him. Often the power of grace preserves secure, a calm within the soul when dangers stand thick around.

Once a lady on a stormy sea, was asked by her companion, "How can you be so calm, when our boat may sink, very soon?" The Christian lady replied, "If you should hold a dagger near my heart, do you think that I would fear, when in your truth and constancy I do confide? Thus in the care of a God of love, I feel that all is right; and life or death, and all the elements He holds in His Almighty power." God often makes His jewels shine, amidst surrounding trials. And among those who fled from savage violence, there was one who bore testimony, in the face of scepticism, of the sealing power and truth of the revealed religion of the Redeemer of a fallen world, before those congregated families. And I fully believe, God will own such an one before His angels.

Again our domestic duties were cheerfully

and faithfully performed. It was ever our desire and aim to have our little family cleanly, comfortable and happy. Just as regularly as I gave my children the food necessary for their existence, that often I taught them to read, or heard them recite what they had learned. And though dark clouds seemed to hang over the fate of the early settlers, and threatened their extinction, yet we could sing of love Divine, and talk with our Father, God.

CHAPTER LII.—MR. G., FLIGHT, LOSS, AND DANGER.

Having walked out into the yard, I saw a man approaching, whom I had never met before. He was rather heavy built, and had a thick dark beard and mustache on his face. He said, "I had a ranch on an old Sante Fee road, and lived ninety miles out from any settlement; friendly Indians told me, that Indians were going to kill me and my family, and advised me to get away with my family very soon." That night, they placed articles for necessity or comfort in their wagon, geared their horses and brought round their steeds; and the wife, a child and a brother, started on a journey, to friends in the state of Missouri. The father remained to try to save property and meet the coming events. After his family had left, he went immediately, to look for his cattle. He found a number shot dead; the rest could not be found. He returned to the house and saw feathers flying in the air; the Indians had been there, they had cut open a feather bed, and shook out the feathers. They had carried off lard, sugar, flour and some other things. Next Mr. Green saw his dog laying shot dead, and as he stood looking around, he heard savage yells of Indians, and fled from his dwelling toward a stream. The Indians pursued him and he told us, "For several hours I saw arrows glittering in the sun, as they were shot towards me, and I dodged them as I fled along the banks of the Cow Creek stream." He was very glad to reach our house and get food.

CHAPTER LIII.— THE THREAT, THE CONCLUSION.

Mr. Green said the Indians had told him, "All the white people on Cottonwood valleys, would be scalped before long." And he said if the Indians came in the country for depradations, they would go straight for the houses in the prairie; and he thought we could hide ourselves from them, and live in some thick timber. He remarked, that "when the Indians had killed persons, they would immediately leave." He said, "Those Indians are accustomed to prairie; they are fearful of harm in the woods." We heard from other sources, that the Indians said, on a certain moon they would scalp every white settler in the country or near the Cottonwood. All persons living near us left the country. Some of them never returned. Mr. Murray wished to put in fall wheat, and said, "If I fail, I will be broke up, and would not know what to do." He went to find his oxen on the prairie; not finding them, he returned, saying, "We shall all be killed; I can't tell where my oxen are, and we have no means of conveyance to get away with. I saw an Indian on a pony, in a skulking manner, near some bushes; and when the Indian saw me, he lay over on the side of his pony, and fled rapidly. I think the Indian was a scout, and others will be in very soon, for murderous purposes." He was painfully excited, saying, "What shall we do?" I said, "I will tell you. You want to put wheat in the field in order that you may have something provided for future necessities. We will go across the Cottonwood, into that heavy thick timber, and will take our stove, cooking utensils, bedding and clothing. We will keep quiet there. You can watch for the Indians as you work."

There was a nice spring in the timber, and we soon carried this into effect. We moved to the woods, and lived there two weeks. We prepared a nice tent to sleep in, with curtains close around, to protect us from the millions of mosquitoes. Mr. Murray worked every day on his land, prepared his ground, and put in wheat. Sometimes I went home at night, and took chickens from their roost, to prepare for our food. We noticed every sound, we hushed every cry or noise from the children, and in case Indians came near our camp, the eldest children were to hide along the brush, and go East as fast as they could, while I carried or helped the youngest along in the same direction. But after two weeks had passed we found there was less prospect of evil to the settlers, and some were now at their homes; accordingly we entered our house as occupants again.

In the woods with hooting owls,
My little children chose to stay;
Lest Indian hatchets—poisoned arrows,
Murderous knives or spears,
Might make a crimson current flow.
And oh! may each dear child
Be safe from the dragon's power,
Beneath the Almighty's shade.

CHAPTER LIV.—THE SOLDIERS, THE INDIANS.

Soon after this there were soldiers out west of us. Their horses were larieted on the grass, and they supposed there were no Indians near; but all at once, when the soldiers least expected, the Indians came with a rush of speed on ponies. They dashed their blankets upward through the air, and at the same time uttered horrid yells, which frightened the soldiers' horses. They broke loose, and the Indians stampeded them off to their own quarters.

There were many Indian warriors west of us. They were seen many hundred strong, and well mounted, but government was now looking a little in that direction; although the progress of war in the States, was making a heavy drain upon the people. About this time, we received intelligence that seventy men were murdered by the savages, on Smokey Hill, in Kansas, in a northwest direction from us, and about seventy-five miles distant. The white settlers generally kept revolvers and guns loaded, in readiness for attack. Yet the defense our home possessed was the strong arm of Providence.

CHAPTER LV.—THE WALK. THE MISSION.

The winter season was at hand. Indians kept more closely in their own quarters. One of Mr. Frank's daughters came to stay with us, and learn to read. She remained for some time for that purpose. She was very pleasant, agreeable company for my children.

One clear cold morning, the appointed time for meeting had rolled around. The air that Sabbath morning was unusually still, the Cottonwood stream was frozen mostly over with ice. The animal we rode would not cross; then I said, "I will be more comfortable walking this cold day. I leave you all to the perusal of books and in the faithful love and care of our heavenly Father, and will go and fill the mission God has given me to prosecute. I crossed on the ice, and when I had walked briskly near the distance of five miles, I arrived at the dwelling of Mr. Wrenfro, where our meetings were held, and found a congregation waiting for my arrival. God always attended those services with the aid of His holy Spirit.

After realizing His special blessing, and partaking of the hospitality those friends were ever anxious to shower upon us, I pursued my course homeward. When I had proceeded to the banks of the Cottonwood, I saw the ice in the center of the stream had broke and washed away, but there was several feet of ice still connected with each shore, and the cold waters dashed along the center of the stream. On the opposite bank, Mr Murray and our three children stood. I walked out on the ice and when about to step into the rolling icy stream, my little boy said, "Oh, ma! oh dear ma!" Then I laughed and sung a happy sacred song. Cheerfulness, and confidential smiles, made our cup of peace full and running over.

CHAPTER LVI PIOUS COUNCIL, WOODEN SHOES.

After a little time, there was a request brought to us, that I should go seven miles below our home, in the Cottonwood valley and hold meeting. Accordingly with Mr. Murray's approbation, I went, and it gave me much strength and help to feel that my companion thought I was in the way of duty. And sure I was in need of the strength, pious council affords.

According to the request of Mrs. Winner, there was meeting at her house; then the appointments were moved from one house to another. And I felt moved to speak from the words contained in the fifteenth chapter of St. John's gospel, the last part of the fifth verse. Namely, "Without me, ye can do nothing." Sometimes the appointments were eight and ten miles distant, and sometimes the dwellings were more than filled. There were several families of French people, that had been brought up in the Catholic faith, but had no priest in that country, and they would come and listen with deep attention, to every word spoken or read. Some would ask me many questions, and I cannot express, how very much I desired, that the clouds which enshrouded souls, might break by the full beams of the Sun of righteousness. At one time the house of Mr. Brenot was filled with persons wishing to hear the gospel, and as many more were attentive listeners in the door-yard. After services, two French ladies came to me and said, "We want you to have a pair of wooden shoes like ours; you would find them very warm and useful." They took my measure, and soon after presented me with a pair of wooden shoes, which I received as a kind token, and preserved them several years as a memento.

CHAPTER LVII.—A DREAM, AN ORGANIZATION.

But with the exception of my husband, I stood alone as to Church fellowship. True we had brought our letters with us from Indiana, but I thought if I could sometimes meet with those who were filled with the Holy Spirit, I would be very much refreshed.

In a dream, I thought I stood in my accustomed place to speak to the people, and read the words of life, in the dwelling of Mr. Wrenfro. I thought an elderly gentleman entered the door of the house, fixed his countenance on me, smiled and looked very happy, walked straight toward me, extended his arm, grasped my hand, and with a cordial welcome, exclaimed, "Sister Murray." The following Sabbath when at their house, I inquired of the family if the father of the representative of that family was a religious man, resembling his son J. W., in features, but a little shorter, and of a very happy temperament. I received an answer in the affirmative; and they also stated, "He was many years a class leader in the Church."

About this time I was strongly impressed

that we must have a Church organization. Accordingly stated that I would then receive names of candidates for membership, and send them to the Church, requesting that ministers might visit us, when God might direct. This invitation for membership, was extended at the close of religious services at the dwelling of Mr. J. Wrenfro, on Cedar Creek, and responded to by several persons, who came forward and filled a bench, that was vacated for the purpose. I wrote the names of each individual, and extended the hand of fellowship. Then asked if any one present, wished to make any remarks. Brother Philip Frank rose, and said, "During a severe affliction, I thought I would die, and promised God, that if he would spare my life I would try to be a Christian; and now with the help of God, I will endeavor to bring those good resolutions, into effect." There was a sacred influence, from the presence of God felt, by all present.

And this is an authentic account of the first Christian organization near Cedar Creek, Kansas. But our duties at home were calling us, and we hastened thither.

CHAPTER LVIII.—DEAR MARY. A MINISTER. A QUARTERLY MEETING.

The duties of the week employed our hands. I gathered wood from the timber, and there, often bowed in prayer. The pathway to the spring, was sacred to me. The several rounds of duties, were cheerfully performed. One evening, after the curtain of night had drawn its sable shades over the face of nature, and Mr. Murray, weary with the toils of the day, had retired to his couch, our dear Mary came to me, with tears rolling down her face, and said, "Oh, ma! pray for me: I want to be a Christian." Mr. Murray rose from his couch, and we all bowed in prayer. We told our dear Mary of Jesus, and the great love of God, and she obtained a hope that evening, that cheered her even in death.

Our William said, "Pray for me," and our little Martha lifted her infant voice in prayer. That week I wrote a letter directing it to the Methodist minister of Emporia. I did not know the name of any religious minister, to which I could write in that country but merely directed in the manner stated. Our letter was sent from Emporia, to brother Roberts, the Cottonwood Falls circuit preacher. He came immediately to visit us, rode up, alighted, and turned to me as I stood near the door, saying, "Sister Murray, I have come in answer to your letter." It was a very happy and welcome reception, of that servant of Christ to our home; and the following day, being Sabbath, we conducted brother R. to Cedar Creek, where he preached a sermon, with which the people were much pleased. The sermon was delivered with unction and Divine Commission. brother R. returned with us to our dwelling, and the following morning left us, for Cottonwood Falls, twenty-five miles distant. He afterwards wrote us a letter stating that in consequence of a severe seige of fever, he had been unable to return to our valley, and invited us to attend a quarterly meeting; and closed the letter with the words: "In the world ye shall have tribulation, but in Christ ye shall have peace."

Our Mary was a very trusty, faithful child, and in my absence could do whatever should be done. Mr. Murray could not attend the meeting, but I could very easily go, and felt that it would be a great privilege. Therefore, I started, the Friday morning before the meeting, taking our little son with us. We traveled on horse-back twenty-five miles, and arrive at the house of Mr. Hinkle, in the town where the meeting was held about the time for evening refreshments. We were given a very friendly welcome, treated with much hospitality, and our horses cared for. That evening we heard an excellent discourse delivered by a faithful servant of Christ. During those meetings, I met with some very excellent, and substantial friends. There I met with brother and sister Gibson, who afterward lived near Marion Center. They were ever faithful, with whom I often met in following years. The love-feast, Sabbath morning, was truly a feast to every Christian present. At the close of a sermon, I presented our letter of Church membership. Well pleased with our journey, Monday evening found us all as a family, at our own dwelling, and everything moving as usual. And we had truly a prayer circle at home.

CHAPTER LIX.—CAPTAIN E. F. ABBOTT KILLED.

One night I had just retired, when I sprang from my couch exclaming, "Father is here." And again I dreamed that I saw Captain E. F. Abbott, my youngest brother, walking with several of his company, their arms around each other's shoulders, my brother appearing prominent—his white wrist-bands and bosom clean and stainless; but a cannon was pointed toward them, and smoke issued from the muzzle. Then I awoke, feeling a deep impression, that we should soon hear sorrowful intelligence.

The following week we received a paper from Goshen, Indiana, stating: "Captain E. F. Abbott has been shot and killed (at Jonesborough, south of Atlanta) in battle, when he was rallying his company for further combat." It was further remarked, that in consequence of his death, "A widowed mother was being brought with sorrow to the grave."

Truly war is a dreadful scourge to any people where its ravages may come, and is contrary to the spirit and teaching of the New Testament. May God quickly roll round that time, when

EVERETT F. ABBOTT.

nations shall learn war no more, but shall beat their swords into plow shares, and spears into pruning hooks; and peace cover the earth, as the waters cover the great deep.

Luther believed, "fire arms the direct suggestion of Satan."

We here quote from an obituary, written from Atlanta, Ga., September 14th, 1864, by W. B. Jacobs.

"Captain Abbott was known as a brave and galliant officer; not by his company alone, but by every officer and man in the regiment. I stood with him the day after Chickamauga, the only captains left in our regiment, by the side of our galliant leader, Col. Baker, as we lay at Rossville, expecting the approach of the enemy. Again, we three stood together on Mission Ridge, on the evening of Nov. 26th, 1863, all unharmed. But when we went into this last charge, our brave leader was not with us, and when the victory was won, I found that of the three, who looked together upon the fields of Chickamauga, and Mission Ridge, I alone was left to see this victory of our brave boys, by which the campaign against Atlanta was ended."

We add,

> Upon the stormy battle field,
>   As victory drew nigh,
> Brave Evriett—honored youth,
>   'Twas his, to bleed and die.

The youngest child, the mother's help and comfort, and only twenty-three years of age. Loved by his company, esteemed by all, was laid silent in the sleep of death, by a ball from the enemy of his country. Is it any wonder that sounds, which the world calls music, should make those hearts heaving with sorrow, feel the wound still deeper? Is it any wonder, that what looks beautiful and grand, to those who never drinked the cup of sorrow, to its dregs should only seem mockery to those who mourn the loss of near and dear friends?

CHAPTER LX.—AFFLICTIONS AND DEATH.

Time rolled onward, and another young lady came to stay at our dwelling that she might be taught in learning.

But Mr. Murray suffered much with disease in his ankles, and was fearful it would result in serious consequences. He could get very little ease, unless his ankles were wrapt in wet cloth, or bathed in water. Therefore I kept them wrapt as he desired, sometimes for weeks together.

One day he said he would like to have medicine from Cottonwood Falls, where the quarterly meeting had been held, and asked if I would ride to the place for that purpose. Accordingly the next morning I started, rode to the town, obtained near as possible what he had requested, and soon as possible returned. The last session of conference, had sent us a preacher, and when Bro. E. visited our dwelling; it was a great entertainment to Mr. Murray, to sit and converse with the pious man. And a hymn which Mr. Murray most delighted to sing commenced thus:

"Come oh! thou traveler unknown,
Whom still I hold, but cannot see."

Several families had moved near as a mile or more distant from us, and they all wished that I should teach school in our house. Mr. Murray said, "It would be all right." Accordingly I commenced school. The children were quite respectful and easily controlled. And if the Caw Indians came in time of school, they would never speak loud.

Mr. Murray's health got no better. If I listened closely, I could hear a rattle on his lungs; his ankles looked better than they had done for a long time, but red, angry looking streaks went upward toward his vitals. He took irregular chills, and a cough became troublesome; I got him cough syrup from Marion Centre, and asked him to have medical advice; but he said he would soon get better and be out attending to his business. I saw that he was getting no better, and dismissed my school. I saw plainly that he was failing in strength, and told him, I feared the syrup done him no good. But he said, it did do him good; it helped to clear his lungs, and when he had used it a little longer, he would be much better in health.

When attending to all that was necessary about the room, my children entered, saying, "Ma, there is wagons coming from toward Cedar Creek, and several men with axes." They entered our timber, and soon wood in large quantities, was stacked near the door-yard. After they had left,

Mr. Murray rose from his couch, looked out the door, and said, "Wal, this beats all."

The friends or neighbors sent us many little dainties, which they thought Mr. Murray might relish. We got him everything he wished, but he could no longer put on his apparal.

A young lady came to help us. I gave her directions about work; and looking round, saw him weeping. I said, "If you have to die, do you feel prepared?" He answered very quickly, "Yes, yes, oh! yes, I am ready—all is right. There is not a cloud on my mind. I have been weighed down with disease for years and could not be what I otherwise would have been. This world is deceitful, it will soon pass away with all persons. We should live for a better world. You have been kind to me. I am glad we were married you must take better care of yourself. It hurts me to talk; it is becoming difficult with my little strength to raise or clear the substance from my lungs. You may send to Marion Centre for the doctor."

A spirited animal stood near the house; my little son was soon passing with speed toward the Centre. He stopped four miles from home and told Mr. Winner, we wished him to go the remaining distance, and bring doctor Rogers, soon as possible. The gentleman's horse stood tied near by, and the doctor was soon at Mr. Murray's bedside. The doctor passed some examination, listened attentively near his lungs; then

I said, "Doctor, tell us the worst of the case—we are prepared for what may come." The doctor shook his head, and said, "I have seen much more flattering cases, I can tell you."

The doctor told me afterwards, that Mr. Murray's lungs were all gone but a small portion of one, and he only gave him medicine to soothe him in his last hours, which I think the doctor surely did, for seeing his breathing was different.

I said, "How do you feel? do you feel very bad? do you suffer much?" He quickly replied, "Oh! no, I do not—all is right now." His afflictions ever had been attended by the utmost patience.

The following day several ladies came to offer assistance, and comfort. A minister, Bro. Earnhart, came in, walked near Mr. Murray's dying couch, and said, "Bro. Murray, are you prepared to die?" Mr. Murray seemed to not hear plainly; but when the question was repeated, he answered quickly, "Oh! yes, yes, all is right—I am ready." And well we might say.

> Not a cloud did arise
> To darken his skies,
> Or hide for a moment,
> His Lord from his eyes.

After the minister left the room, Mr. Murray lay quiet for some time, we watched him closely, and anticipated every want; but it became necessary that I should for one minute go to the opposite side of the room: I quickly returned. Mrs. Winner stood by his bedside, and remarked, "Those large drops of sweat on his forehead are cold." Then I saw, that he was gazing upward. I called his name many times, but when I saw that he would not speak again to me in this world, I bowed near the bed-side, but soon rose and saw that his eyes were nearly closed.

His mortal life had passed away.
Angels had come, the vain world fled,
Bright glory immortal, had dawned on his view.

Mr. Murray had been truly a friend to all that was benevolence, righteousness and honor; not in words only, but in active deeds, and he had gone to reap the reward of those that are righteous in the sight of God—saved by the washing of regeneration. Yet his lonely family were still in the vale of tears. Heavily the clouds of sorrow burst over our heads. That one who for more than fourteen years, had been our counselor and help mate, had left for those climes, where sorrow never enters. I and my children were left to weep. But my children said to me, "Mother, your health is failing; you must stop this deep grief, or we shall soon have no mother." I knew from my own feeling, this would be the case, and tried to look forward to that time when friends will meet in heaven. But when I and my children were returning from meeting held on

Cedar Creek, and arrived in sight of our home that had been cheered by the presence of our companion, and father, we all as a lonely band burst into a flood of tears. I have more than once since then, remarked to my children. "O! if your father could have remained with us, just to sit in his chair, and give us council or advice; and for the benefit of his society, it would have been a blessing of great magnitude. But another tie was in heaven, and in prayer we felt power, and sacred drawing toward the better land.

Time is short at the longest—a hand's breadth—an age is as nothing when compared with eternity, yet God is an abiding friend; and God still granted us, in the midst of every trial, the witness of His Holy Spirit that He was our friend and help. And like a tree in open prairie, we were upheld while blasts of adversity swept around us.

CHAPTER LXI.—FAMILY AFFLICTIONS. BROTHER F. AND DAUGHTER.

It was in the spring of the year when Mr. Murray passed away to a home in heaven. And Mr. Wrenfro sent his son to plow three acres of land, which I undertook to cultivate with the hoe. When the work was partially accomplished, my boy nine years of age, fell and dislocated his elbow-joint, injuring and and splintering the bones badly; and soon after my daughter Mary became sick with fever. But thanks be to a compassionate heavenly Father, we were brought through those afflictions, and were again enabled to meet with those who met for the service of God. When we had been providentially detained, Bro. Philip Frank, had given a helping hand to the work, and opened and closed Sabbath-school with prayer. At this we were much rejoiced, and desired Bro. Frank to act as superintendant in time to come.

Bro. F. was loved and esteemed as a citizen—he was well fitted for that capacity.

About this time, a lovely daughter of Bro. F. was taken very suddenly sick with congestion of the lungs, and only lived a very short time. Soon after the attack, she said, "I am going to die." Her last words were, "Jesus is coming, he is coming."

When the society on Cedar Creek was first formed, this young lady had come forward, and added her name to the list of those who desired to serve God; and now King Jesus, the immortal glorious Jesus, had come and received her to Himself. Though her friends were left to mourn, yet their loss was her gain.

Time was passing onward, and it became necessary that I should go to Cottonwood Falls on business. Therefore, leaving everything at home the best arranged possible, I went, taking my little son, who always attended me, when called to leave our home on business. There was no one to share the burden of care; I now had all to bear. On leaving home, I employed some one to remain with the children left at home.

Sometimes we had to go to Plymouth, forty miles, for milling, and sometimes to Emporia, fifty miles distant. At one time when returning, we had to stop and remain over night.

We stopped at the house of an elderly gentleman, a deacon in the Baptist Church. They had a protracted meeting in progress. Near the hour of service, I put on my bonnet to attend the family; Deacon Beverly, Preacher R., and Deacon Williams, walked near and united in saying, I should "speak first in the services." Bro. R. said he would follow. From a sence of duty, and from request, I felt bound to comply, opened my Testament, and the words contained in part of the eleventh verse of the 22 chapter of Revelations, were presented as a subject for remarks. The words, "He that is unjust let him be unjust still." Then Bro. R. followed with remarks on the five first verses, of the same chapter. The hospitality of brother and sister Beverly, has been very abundant toward me, and my family. May God bless the many dear friends, who have displayed true Christian kindness. The blessed Savior has said, "Whosoever giveth a cup of water only in the name of a disciple, shall not loose his reward." I and my children bowed daily together, in unison worshipped our Savior and Redeemer, and on rising in the morning, I walked directly to the door, looking upward, felt truly to adore the Giver of all peace and blessing. We felt consolations which those who know not God cannot fathom.

But we often heard rumors of Indian troubles. My children were sometimes frightened, and thought they saw Indians in the distance. Mr. Murray had commenced a house on our homestead, which—with some assistance from my mother, who came to visit us—was prepared for a dwelling. I taught a school in the house—a three months term, not long after entering it as a dwelling. I also taught three months in a log school-house, on the opposite side of the Cottonwood River, from our dwelling. The following season a school trustee came and offered good wages, and said, the neighborhood would help me in different ways if I would move three miles distant and teach their school. We moved to the place, bought a Sabbath-school library, taught the day school, and kept up Sabbath-school, through all the pleasant seasons of that year.

CHAPTER LXII. —GRASSHOPPERS. FLIGHT FROM SAVAGES.

During an intermission of school, my scholars said, "Oh! teacher, come and look, there are many little creatures moving between us and the sun, they make a shadow like a cloud on the earth." As we stood looking, they commenced to settle round us thickly on weeds, bushes and grass. Grasshoppers in vast numbers, covered all vegetation.

The heavy drouth that year had already injured the corn crop; and now grasshoppers were sweeping the sustenance from the remains of vegetation.

But our school was still progressing when word came, that Indians from west of us, were coming in that direction, Indian warriors four hundred strong, committing depradations as they came. They had often threatened destruction to the settlers, and now all persons for miles around, were rushing toward the Centre, to take refuge in the Court House. Our little family and articles necessary for our comfort, was taken into a wagon and with the crowd we entered the commodious rock building. A rock wall which now stands, was not then built; but the men brought their wagons round in a circle, to delay the progress of the Indians, in order that the white men might gain advantage. There were a goodly number of volunteer soldiers, come to our assistance, or protection. They stationed men with revolvers in hand, about the door of the house, expecting an attack, and sent men to find out what the Indians were doing.

There was a Doctor Rogers with the company of scouts. He had a spy glass and a fleet horse; he trusted to the fleetness of his horse, and delayed some time, watching the movements of the Indians, after the rest were returning. The Indians saw him, and tried to cut off his retreat. Then came a race for life, as the Indians had fleet horses; the doctor put spurs to his horse, and with the greatest exertions possible, barely made his escape.

The Indians robbed, killed stock and plundered considerably. They knew the white people were prepared for them at the Center, and did not enter the town, but took their course toward Council Grove. Soldiers were in that town, and the Indians did not wish an encounter. They went to the Caw Reserve and had a battle with the Caws. The Caws were victorious; then those savage Indians, through fear of being pursued, separated into small bands, and fled in different directions. But those persons at Marion Center, were in ignorance for some time, as to the course the Indians were pursuing; and as there were not provisions at the Center, to keep so many persons, they started in wagons, and on horseback, went to Cottonwood Falls thirty-five miles farther east. They hurried forward, soldiers riding along the sides of the procession, not knowing what moment they might hear the horrid war whoop, or see the murderous steel descend on the helpless ones, or feel a death wound inflicted. The few soldiers were unskilled in warfare and all might have been easily overpowered. But we at last arrived in the town, and took refuge in a large rock school-house. We found the citizens of that place in a state of excitement.

I heard one man in high standing in society remark, "It would be a blessing to the world if the savages were all exterminated." We remained in that town, till we heard of the Indians, proceedings. The settlers then returned to their homes and occupations.

When our school was closed in the fall of the year, I and my children moved to our own home.

CHAPTER LXIII.—SEVERE WINTER, LOSS.

The following winter many hundreds of cattle died. The settlers said, "Perhaps the grasshoppers had poisoned the grass." They had surely injured the strength or amount of sustenance in it.

A more severe winter than usual followed, and instead of a mild winter and early spring, that is usual in Kansas, winter was protracted beyond its usual period; and when the boom, boom, of the prairie fowl, or the notes of the prairie lark should have saluted our ears, storms of snow, sleet and wind, fell pitiless on the cattle of Kansas. Weaker than usual, a protracted winter they could not endure. Dead cattle lay along the banks of streams more than could easily be numbered; many had slipped down creek banks, powerless to extricate themselves, had perished. Others from weakness, were incapable of rising when down; the sleet and storms finished their existence.

A widow lady not far from us, owned one hundred head. They all died but just one. Mr. Murray had secured a few cattle; they had increased to about thirty-four, and that winter sixteen of our cattle died. I had traded for a few sheep, and lost fourteen lambs, that season. The fall previous I took seventy-five dollars worth of seed wheat of the treasurer of the school district in which I had taught: it was poorly put in the ground by one to whom we had rented, and the following harvest, I did not receive the value of the seed in grain.

Our improved land was rented constantly, and I was to receive one third of each crop, with the exception of the year, when I found seed wheat, I was to receive the half of the crop.

CHAPTER LXIV.— CULTIVATION, DROUTHS, GRASSHOPPERS.

I think if small grain is put in the ground at the proper season, and rightly put in, it is a very sure crop in Kansas, or in most parts at least; but on such bottom land, if put in late, thereby not obtaining good root in the earth, or if put in carelessly, or too little seed, the sunflowers which seem natural to the soil, shoot above the grain, causing it to blast. I never knew a crop of rye to fail in Kansas. But corn crops have often failed from drouths late in the season. Therefore corn in that country, should be put in the ground very early in the spring; the first of April is not too soon in that country, as a general rule, and makes much better corn, than the later seasons of planting.

Often new settlers in that country, have been too poor to buy seed wheat, got their corn in late, and received no crops. On high land, a dry season would cause greater damage. Partly from ignorance of the proper season for farming, and partly from other causes, Kansas has suffered much. One year I remember traveling a few miles over prairie. The spring wheat had dried up too short for binding, fall or winter wheat had done better; but corn was quite short on upland, and grasshoppers had stripped all the leaves from the stalks. But the cane fields stood fresh and green. Grasshoppers do not generally disturb sugar cane, and drouth does not easily harm it. The year which I just mentioned, there was much suffering from lack of the necessaries of life. A committee of ladies was sent out from the town of Marion Center, then our county seat, to find out the suffering ones; and among others in lack of necessities of life, they found a sick woman, and her little babe eleven days old. All the nourishment she had received during that time, was merely bran bread.

Let us consider when we have all that is required for the strengthening of our mortal bodies; those things which are palatable and nice, are we just as thankful, and do we love the great Giver of all good, just as much as we should do? May God help us to be thankful, and forbid that we should live as the beasts that perish; but heirs to an immortal crown may our souls bow before the throne of Deity in thankful adoration.

But to return to the subject of our rented land; I did not receive more than enough to pay our taxes, taking one year with another. Some years we received very little or nothing and our family we surely felt must be comfortable. Therefore our stock often had to be sold, to get money to pay taxes; while we retained the products of the field for our home provisions.

CHAPTER LXV.—MRS. GREEN'S STORY.

But hark, I hear a sound of voices: two ladies are at the door. Mrs. Green, whose husband had fled from the Indians, had returned, bringing her mother with her from Missouri. They remained at our dwelling for some hours, and Mrs. G. related scenes that took place while she lived on Cow Creek. She stated that "A train going to Texas, passed that way, and a young man belonging to the train, shot a squaw, killing her. Then Indians came round the train, and said, if the man who killed their squaw was not given up to them, they would kill every one on the train: the man had to be delivered over to the will of the savages; then they commenced with his forehead, turning the scalp back, and cut all the hide from his body." Thus she said, "He was skinned alive." The muscles of the woman's face, and excitement while relating this, showed how terrible the scene appeared to her.

Mrs. G. also stated, that while she lived at the same ranch, "An Indian, while drunk, inserted his butcher knife into the body of his squaw, so that some of her intestines protruded. The other Indians replaced them, sewed up the wound, and the squaw recovered."

After this recital, Mr. Green entered, and stated, that when the Indians wished to rob trains, they would at night, get under or near the wagons; and at the first movments at dawn, kill the unsuspecting travelers.

But those persons took their departure from our dwelling; and a diversity of cares, time engaged, and onward fled the hours.

CHAPTER LXVI.—PRAIRIE FIRE, A DISTRESSING SCENE.

I have sometimes had occasion to ride a good sized animal, through prairie grass on rich bottom land, where the grass was above my head when on horse-back. Persons that never saw such prairie grass may wonder at this, and if they should see a fire in dry grass of this description, at night especially, they would remember it a long time.

Our neighbor, E. Smith, informed us that he had just been out West all alone, watching the Indians and trying to find horses, which the Indians had stolen from him. He was then on his return home; but when near a bend of the Arkansas, where two streams met, he had witnessed a distressing scene. Many horses belonging to the Indians, were congregated together, and surrounded by burning flames. The prairie grass being extremely high and heavy, there was no means of escape; and he said, "Such rearing, plunging, and biting of the suffering, dying animals in the burning flames, he never would wish to witness again.

The soil in Kansas is generally rich; and heavy growths of grass are yearly spread over the country. When the grass, dried by the rays of a summer sun or drying winds of fall, ignite with the flames of an Indian, or travelers' camp fire; or, as in the past purposely set by revengful Indians, such a fire swept onward by strong wind, has often roused the sleeping pioneer, in the late hours of night, by the glare of flame, to behold his granries and out-buildings being consumed. Some have lost their dwelling by this means. One man not far from us, lost his life in trying to save his property from the devouring element.

When there were no roads, nothing but Indian trails, there was much trouble from those fires. Persons acquainted with the country, can arrange preventatives, against the occurrence of such calamities. But to one who fears nothing from the consuming flame, the sight of those long lines of fire, rolling from valley to hill, and extending from one assent to another, sometimes appearing as an extensive sea of fire, at times a darkness of smoke preceeding the same; then the brilliancy of reflection on the sky, and flash of extending flame, and the cracking of burning weeds, in the midst of progressing, rising, and sometimes towering flames, would appear as truly grand; though such a sight, always filled my mind, with anxious thought and sympathy for the distressed.

CHAPTER LXVII.—SENSE OF DUTY, THE SICK.

I was often called on to visit the sick, during several years, when physicians were distant. Ministers of the gospel preached at stated periods, yet they were often distant; and I was sometimes requested to attend to religious services, on funeral occasions. From a sense of duty I complyed; and felt that I had merely filled a servant's place, and done my heavenly Father's bidding. Once when requested, I failed to go; I felt some indisposition as to health, yet ever afterward regretted the failure. I cannot regret serving God fully; we are dust, yet our heavenly Father loves us still.

The circuit preacher requested me to hold and fill an appointment on the Cottonwood valley; but my cares were many. He said, "Riding would be beneficial to your health, and less toil more for your good." Yet I thought of the language once addressed to Timothy: "Take charge of the Church till I come." And I let the work rest altogether on the responsibility of Bro. T. S.

CHAPTER LXVIII. FOUR SAVAGES: "WHERE IS WHITE MAN?"

I and my youngest child were one still, quiet day sitting alone in our dwelling; when four large, wild looking, dark savages rode up to the door, calling out, "Where is white man?" I said, "White men are at work." They looked at each other and laughed, then rode off in the direction where our horses ranged. My little girl started to watch the fate of the horses; my anxiety for my child gave wings to my speed, and I soon arrived where two men were preparing cane works; their horses saddled and bridled stood near. Those men taking a short cut across, got so near the Indians that they swam the river in their flight; but they took with them a horse belonging to one of the men who had pursued them. My little girl soon returned, bringing our horses with her.

The family of Mr. H., had left our part of the country, and another of superior qualities, moved into the same dwelling. This family was composed of Mr. and Mrs. Brown, and two little girls.

CHAPTER LXIX.—FIVE INDIANS, STOLEN HORSES.

A few months after their arrival in our country, Mr. B. was afflicted with an intermitting fever. His faithful wife, business like and true, had fed and tied their horses of fine appearance, in full view of the door where her husband usually placed them. After this arrangement for the night had been made, five savage looking Indians came to the door and wished to stay in the house that night. Mrs. B. gave them to understand that her family was sick; and motioned them to stay in an old log hut. They set down on the ground not far from the horses, and near one end of the log building. Mrs. B. then told her husband, "Our horses will be taken by the Indians this night." When all was quiet and the evening hours were fast passing, Mrs. B. still kept a little aperture of opening at the door, and remained listening at the sound of the feeding animals; as they made good use of the new mown hay. Soon she said, "Mr. Brown, our horses are gone!" He then sprang from his couch, started out, then turned and took his revolver; the Indians were still in sight, mounted on his horses, and part walking. He did not shoot or speak. The moon was shining, he pursued closely after them, as they went along the valley toward the house of Mr. Creamer. The gentleman and a young man his son, had just returned late from a ride, and were preparing to leave their horses for the night; when Mr. Brown called out with the highest tones of voice he could command. "Indians! Indians! save your horses." Then the Indians fled precipitately from sight. But soon whoops or yells resounded in the night air, then other Indians on the opposite side of the stream above our house, yelled again, and their savage yells were answered by Indians, in the valley below near the stream, and by others back on the hills. In this manner they apprized each squad of Indians, that the white people were aware of their proceedings. It was well for my children, that they were so closely locked in slumber, that although wakened by the dismal sounds, they scarcely knew what the omen might be, till our neighbors hurried to our dwelling; then we found that our horses had been stolen. Two good animals and a colt that had been placed not far from the house for the night, were gone. Two other horses belonging to a neighbor, living at that time on our land were taken.

The Indians stole about thirty head of horses that night; and would have taken twice that number, if the white people had not become aroused to the knowledge of their deeds. Two of our neighbors rode rapidly to the dwellings of Mr. J. and M. Rigs, who kept much stock on hand, and were well prepared for encounter with the Indians; a number of white men were soon collected and followed the Indians in a south-west direction, guided partialy by their tracks. After two days they saw a large Indian ride our mare up to a ranch, our colt peculiarly marked by natural white spots, walking by her side. By this means, they soon found where more of the horses were, but the Indians wished to kill the white men, and were only kept from bloodshed, violence and cruelty, by their chief. They drew their weapons and placed a revolver at Mr. Brown's breast. Their chief came that moment near, and at the word of command they withdrew their threatened violence.

The Indians were anxious for fight; then their chief said, "Pay the Indians money, then they will give up the horses." Accordingly the white men paid the required sums, and got part of the horses. For one of my horses they paid seven dollars, and for another six. One of our horses was so badly injured by a nail of an Indian saddle, that the animal was nearly useless for riding ever afterward, and one of Mr. Brown's horses wos so badly injured, that it was of little account.

The Indians told the white men, "If you had not found us out quick, we would have got many more horses, and we will yet steal all back, and take many more." Therefore, our horses were very closely secured with chains and padlocks; and the slightest sound or movement at night, I would be on my feet, looking out for Indians.

One moonlight night a man rode up and called out to us. "Take care of your horses; Indians have been seen round; soldiers are looking for them." But the Indians never molested our horses again.

CHAPTER LXX.—SIX SERPENTS.

With a request, I here comply, for one said to me, "Tell us about serpents." I thought I would pass these little stories ore.

But when not far from my house, I cleaned wheat; two of my little children were seated under the shadow of a stack. I worked, and screened, and filled the sacks of wheat. Soon the children stepped before me, pale and speechless, started in to their mother's face; then pointed where they had been seated. There upon the ground, a monstrous serpent lay. I got a lengthy stake, and when it was dispatched, my children their story told. They said, "It came toward us rolling in the form of hoop, and when we jumped away, it struck the stack, then straightened and slowly went to creep away." Although it was large, it was not of the boa's dimensions, yet to my children it had threatened death.

And once my eldest daughter stooped to dip sparkling water from beneath the shadow of rocks, when something struck her bonnet; then she hastily withdrew. But a quick glance displayed six serpent's heads protruding; and spiteful tongues arrayed, just above where she had stooped to dip the cooling draught; and when she turned to leave the place, a lengthy rattle snake with poison fangs, did strike her dress. The child's call brought aid, and the venomous reptile was slain.

Once my little boy was playing hide and seek, when looking wild and strange, he stepped quite near and said, "Ma, in the dark place where I hid, there is a large cold ring of iron." Then I looked and there, still in a serpents coil a large reptile lay; but soon it was powerless, made, and carried from the place.

When I was walking near low pasture ground, a child ran forward in a path, but quickly she returned, and said, "Oh, ma, don't you hear that noise!" And sure it was very plain, and the sound was like telegraphic wire in its vibrations. The child said, "It is a serpent just behind those bushes, and it is very large." The child ran and brought a stake. Though a little fearful of the consequences, I hesitated not to strike a blow. Then its large jaws it threw extended wide and a cotton mouth displayed. I backward jumped, then forward stepped the battle to renew, and when it was gained, we onward walked along the path.

Of reptiles, I might tell more, but this will sure suffice. In the country new, near rocky quarries or low lands, near groves and streams, it surely was not strange, that reptiles should abound. And taking it for granted that the lady who requested this account, has given us permission, we will pass to tell a little story which in mirth was ended.

CHAPTER LXXI. THE CHILDREN'S FRIGHT.

One evening my children said, "Mother there surely is an Indian standing on the hill above the house; the horses will be stolen, or we might be killed." Then I said, "I will go and find him out." Accordingly, I took a pitch-fork and went confronting the frightful foe; but lo! a gentle colt allowed me to walk up and place my hand upon his side. Then I returned and laughed about the apparition.

And a moral we find. Imaginary evils often prove only blessings in disguise.

CHAPTER LXXII.—A TEXAS OX. DANGER.

The trifle I have just related, brings to mind, that which for the moral I will sketch. A wild and dangerous Texas ox was ranging round our yards, and would chase any person, if it saw them out side the fence. A cattle herder on a trained horse, which would jump away whenever the animal went to gore his side, and then a large black braided leather whip, with quickness he applied; but still he failed to keep the animal away.

A lady stopping at our house, went out with just a club in hand; I called, "You will be killed;" but she with careless air went on. When I saw the threatened danger, I ran between the woman and the foe. When it turned at me, I struck the tines of a pitch-fork, with all my strength, into his smoking nostrils. Still he onward came till I had backed against a fence; then his fury tore the fork tines from his bleeding nose, and his long horns struck by each side of my body on the fence; then quick I yelled, at the sound he whirled; and very soon the fence a safeguard proved.

Now the moral we will consider. If persons meddle with other people's frays, often hate, or danger tries its power upon the party last engaged. Therefore, judgment, and caution ever should direct our ways, while peace and kindness still are written on our souls.

CHAPTER LXXII. INDIAN JOHNSON, A WILD PONY, INDIANS.

Time was flitting with a busy wing, I and my children in their western home, when Indian Johnson entered and received an offered seat; he set in silence for sometime, then a train of Indians was seen approaching, and first of all the train, a young squaw nearly white rode up, with a child in her arms. Johnson arose immediately, saying, "That my squaw; I have two squaws now. One Indian died, then I took his squaw." Johnson's first squaw came next, with two papooses on the pony which she rode. They all bowed in recognition; then the trail of Caw Indians passed on.

There is considerable difference of shade in the complexion of different tribes, but coarse straight black hair is their inheritance. The young Caw Indians seemed very regardless of cold, and would ride their ponies in most extreme weather destitute of any clothing.

When the Indians wished to break a wild pony for use, they would sometimes strap a young Indian fast to the animal's back, giving the youngster the bridle rein. They put this process in operation at one time; the pony was ungovernable and the young Indian strapped to the pony, instead of remaining on its back, got turned to the under side and was very soon killed.

Indians still passed our home, when going to and fro on buffalo hunts; squaws leading the pack horses, and carrying papooses on ponies. They often dragged tent poles attached to the sides of their ponies; Indian men carrying guns and other weapons, ready for hunting excursions; also carrying polecats, beavers, muskrats, or whatever game they might have found, excepting the heavier game that was carried on their ponies. The Indian cahoot, with feathers sticking in their hair, was to strangers yet a novelty. But no more white men's scalps, were carried by our door as there had once been in former days. The country was being settled rapidly, and Indian visits becoming less and less frequent. The Indians had often set our prairies on fire, but now well traveled roads and fields, served for some protection. And I can look back to the time when I and my little son worked so rapidly, pulling big grass, and burning against a coming fire, that blood filled my mouth, the circumstances with me never to occur again.

CHAPTER LXXiV.—MILLING EXPEDITION, MR. GIBSON.

Milling expeditions, and for trade at Cottonwood Falls, Plymouth and Emporia, after Mr. Murray had been taken from us, had been my lot, and that of my little son.

We once met Mr. Gibson, when he was returning from mill, he walked qickly in front of his team and with a friendly shake of the hand, he said, "You must visit my family at Marion Center." We had become acquainted at a quarterly meeting, and our families were ever sincere friends.

Brother and sister Gibson stood alone for several years as Christians in frontier life. But soon, Bro. Gibson passed to that home beyond these mortal shores, where Mr. Murray had first arrived, while their families were still left on the sea of life; but our frail barge is drawing nearer and nearer the port of rest in heaven; and though the waves roll high and boistrous, yet we are securely resting on that Almighty arm, whose love and faithfulness, will soon bring us, where friends shall part no more.

CHAPTER LXXV.—SISTER BROWN, A LETTER, POETRY.

And there is another dear sister, namely, Maria Brown; who with her companion, and two children, came to live about a mile from our dwelling, soon after the time of Mr. Marray's death. She was a faithful friend, pious, sincere, sympathetic, benevolent and active in all good deeds; she was a faithful steward in the Methodist Church for about eight years. And now her two daughters, names are wrote in the Church militant, and we hope to meet in the triumphant Church above. And may the companion of that sister in Christ, who is now trusting in the saving power of his Redeemer, be at last numbered with the faithful, near the throne of God in glory. And if sister B. should ever look upon these lines, she will remember the many times we have bowed in unison, before the throne of mercy both in congregations where saints have met, and in retirement where none but God could hear, those fervent prayers we have uttered in behalf of loved ones;, and we have unitedly felt salvation's current flow, and drinked of the fountain of life, which lifted us far above the unrest, which those feel who know not God.

All things of a worldly nature is perishing, but God is immutable; his words of promise, firm as the throne of Deity.

Since writing the above lines, I have received a letter from the sister just mentioned, a portion of which I will here insert.

FLORENCE, MARION CO., KANSAS, May 12, 1879.

Dear sister Murray, your very welcome letter is at hand. I hope and pray that you may enjoy more and more of God's love, and may his smile cheer you continually; I know from blest experience, that we shall be extremely happy, if we trust in Him, and follow closely in the footsteps of our blessed Savior; even if we do have many things to try us here; and cannot understand why we are placed just where we are; yet if we only trust in Him, we shall come off more than conquerors, through Him that has loved us. For we do know that God's promises were never yet broken; and He has said, He will never leave or forsake us.

Sister Murray, I have been so very happy since our protracted meeting at Cedar Point, I cannot express my happiness. The sweet joy that I feel continually, it is a holy joy beyond measure. I wish all might feel as I do. I want to pray all the time. Yes, sister Murray, I know you understand this, for you have told me your experience, in happy days gone by. May our heavenly Father ever comfort you with the sweet influence of His Holy Spirit. May your pathway be illuminated by His smiles, and if we are not permitted to meet again on earth, I trust we shall meet in heaven.

The following lines I respectfully address to sister Murray.

When the sinking sunbeams lie
On the forest branches high,
And the hour of prayer draws nigh,
    Remember me.

When the cares of day are gone,
And the pensive hour steals on,
And with my God I am alone,
    I will remember thee.

When the quiet moonbeams bright,
Tinge the clouds with silvery light,
May the cross appear in sight;
    His love encompass thee.

When our days on earth are ore,
And we reach the shining shore;
There we will shout, and sing His praise
    Through all eternity.

MARIA BROWN.

CHAPTER LXXVI.—MINISTER'S VISIT. A NEW DWELLING.

Brother Roberts, the first regular minister that ever came up the Cottonwood Valley to proclaim the gospel, whom I attended to an appointed place of worship on Cedar Creek, again visited our home on his way to Marion Center, to fill the place of a presiding elder. I again accompanied him on horse-back, meeting with sister Gibson, and other dear friends, whom I may never see again, till we shall sing earth's trials ore, around the great white throne.

After Mr. Murray was called to his home on high, many cares crowded around me. I labored faithfully and diligently that my children might be supplied with all of earth's comforts. I hired the breaking of fifteen acres of land; also more fencing made and reset, and for a while, we surely had prosperity.

The roof of the cabin on our homestead had not been made of durable timber, and was not water proof; therefore, I felt the necessity of a new building; I arranged for lumber and got it on hand; but shingles I could not get without going seventy miles, and bringing them in a wagon; therefore, I and my son went to Junction

City, and paid seven dollars a thousand, bringing home the required amount.

The carpenters were employed, business moved rapidly, and we soon were occupants of a comfortable lath and plastered dwelling. But in the midst of cares, I did not wish to wander from my heavenly Father; I desired to live near His throne of mercy; I laid my Bible near my couch, and immediately after rising, would kneel and read words of consolation and comfort.

For years I had been specially blest, (when there was no intruder near) on rising from our rest, by going immediately into the open air, and worshiping Him whose designs and handy work is seen in all created things; and while the untutored Indian, sees God in the clouds, and hears him in the wind, shall modern skeptics say there is no God, and show a weakness of reasoning powers, equal to those heathen who say, "The earth rests upon an ox, and the ox stands upon an elephant?" But there are some whose eyes may rest on these pages, who know the power of a God of love, and free grace, to bless and teach, and guide into all truth; those who desire to know his councils. The blessed Savior who has magnified the law, and made it honorable, reaches down the power of grace, to lift us to the skies, and whosoever will accept, may receive the elevating knowledge of Divine favor. And God has said by the mouth of inspiration. "In the day thou seekest me with all thy heart, I will be found." He has never told us to seek His face in vain; His promise is immutable. "As the mountains are round about Jerusalem, so the Lord is round about those that fear Him." As a child would love and fear to grieve or disobey a most worthy parent; thus let us regard our heavenly Father.

Those who deep in their inmost souls possess this filial fear, are heirs to an immortal crown. And He has commanded us to call on Him while He may be found;" and those that come unto Him, He will in no wise cast out. He is no respecter of persons; He seeth not as man seeth, but is a discerner of the thoughts and intents of the heart.

CHAPTER LXXVII.—A BROKEN TIE. MARY'S DEATH.

A flitting sunbeam, or a pleasing dream,
Are quickly past, and we are left to weep;
The rose bud broke by ruthless hands;
A spring flower faded in an hour,
And broken ties; and deathlike forms,
Our hearts must wring with pain;
But Christ is conqueror over death;
And God who is the resurrection, and the life,
Can heal each broken heart,
And cheer with hope Divine.

My dear Mary was surely a very lovely, trusty, noble child. I taught her to read when she was very young; study was ever her delight; she boarded away from her own home, and went to school about five months, and became acquainted with a man of position and influence. She married at the early age of sixteen, and after one year of married life, she went to try the realities of eternity.

But oh! the circumstances were painfully-heart rending. She said, "Oh mother I know I shall die." She wished to stay with her lovely babe, that was two weeks old at the time of her death. She said, "O if I could live just a few years; but I know I shall die; I wish I had loved God more: I am too weak for much; but I can look up, and trust in God; all my hope and trust is in God now."

Sister Gibson and myself bowed by her bedside in prayer, then a smiling heavenly radiance lit up her countenance making her seem almost angelic. The doctor said she was better; then her husband said, "O, Mary I am so glad; kiss me, my Mary." Then for the last time, she imprinted a kiss on her husband's face.

Soon we saw the destroyer, death was near. She said, "Bring my babe that I may see it; then she said, "I am blind, I cannot see it, hold it near." She felt its face and arms, then said, "That will do." Soon the death rattle commenced; she tried to talk, saying, "Mother, mother, mother." But her tongue became so useless by death, that she could not articulate the words she wished to speak; and when to all human appearance, she had ceased to live, her husband, myself and younger daughter, commenced to weep aloud.

Then circumstances of unusual occurrence took place. Our Mary whose tongue had seemed useless by death, spoke aloud in a pleasant lively tone, saying, "What is the matter?" Then all was silent, and still in death. This was surprise indeed, which caused us to remain for some time perfectly silent.

When Mary had called my name, and could not converse for mortification, and death held her in its cruel grasp. I said to her, "Jesus will go with you, Mary." And I feel sure with the ransomed ones, she doth a smiling angel stand, whispering, Mother, you and my dear child will come soon.

But who can feel as a mother can; and sure there never was a more lovely daughter, than my own dear Mary. Nature had given her a form of perfect loveliness. Her delicate little feet I went to kiss, but they had clothed them with habilaments for the grave.

She had much the features of her father; and the same dark hazel eyes. Often I have seen her climb up on her father's lap; but now those mortal frames were still in death. They laid her in her coffin, and were about to close the lid for the last time, then my impulse of the moment was to stop the sexton's work when just as quick as wings of thought, and impressed deep on the very soul, these words, "I am the resurrection and the life," so changed my course of action, that I spoke aloud, "God can open that coffin."

And surely those numbered with the dead, God's power to immortality can bring, for Omnipotent Almighty power to Him alone belongs.

The little girl my daughter left, is the image of her mother; and now in Marion County, Kansas. Seven summers have passed over her infant head. May the angels of love and protection throw around her their balmy wings, and guide her securely, and wisely, till she meets her dear mother, where death shall never enter, and God will wipe away all tears from the faces of the ransomed. Surely there is nothing firm but heaven. Christ says: "Set not your affections on things on earth, but on things in heaven, where moth and rust cannot corrupt, nor thieves break through and steal."

Afflictions multiplied, surely surrounded me; but God brings us safe through floods, and flames, to dwell with those to whom it is given, to be arrayed in fine linnen, clean and white, at the marriage supper of the Lamb. Surely they that trust in the Lord, shall be as Mount Zion, which cannot be removed.

CHAPTER LXXVIII. MY CHILDREN'S LOSS, A RAILROAD, BOARDERS.

My little son who was ambitious and sensative, though a slender child, had tried to help his mother in many things, but I let him go from me, with the hope of his gaining more education. He remained with his Grand mother one year, and should have prosecuted his studies further, before returning. But when he returned, a railroad had found its way up our valley, and a rush of emigration, was flooding our country, and there were many, whose influence was not for the best in our land. And the loss, which my children had met in the death of their father, was bitterly felt by me, their widowed mother, and more than once have I heard deep regret for mistakes of youth, and may God throw around such in following years, His almighty protection. I and my youngest child Martha, struggled with toil and care; she took much from my hands, in care of stock, and charge of work. Once when I was sick, her care of me and all else, caused her a serious illness. But time changes things of an earthly nature. The busy hum of enterprise and life saluted our ears, and a railroad conductor, Mr. O'Bryen, requested us to "board sixteen employees, while they worked two weeks, at grade work." After a little consideration, I entered upon the duties of the same. Those persons, we had consented to board were very civil. I read daily from the Bible, in their presence, supplicated the blessing of almighty God to rest on all present; and sometimes, when I had retired, to another part of the dwelling, I could hear them reading the Bible. They spent every evening in singing very nice religious hymns. Two of the young men had been trained in the midst of pious surroundings.

A minister visited us, and we had preaching at our dwelling; some persons from a camp in the timber near, came to listen, and there was quite an audience. But near three weeks passed onward, and another conductor, Mr. Malady, entered our home, and requested that twenty-one persons, should get their board at our residence, while the butments of a railroad bridge, was being built. I complied with the request, and in five weeks cleared one hundred dollars of all expences. The stone-masons, and the contractor, took quarters in a part of our dwelling. Mr. Malady, who employed the workmen, was a true gentleman, though a Catholic. One of the masons was a Methodist, and one was a Baptist. The common work-men quartered in a temporary building built for the purpose, and just came in for their meals. One day a new hand was added, and then another. The two new-commers, were looked upon suspiciously by the rest of the hands, and one person requested me, to take charge of seventy-five dollars, saying, "I am fearful I will be robbed." This I kept for him till the day he left. On that day, I handed the roll to him, requesting him to count it, which he did in my presence; he then thanked me for the care of the same.

The first time one of the last boarders came in our dwelling to dine I noticed him speake very roughly to the workmen, that were in the room, and I resolved to speak to him of his rough ways. Accordingly, the next meal time, when he commenced to speak wickedly I said, "Harry, you are the first person that ever said such wicked words in my house." Then Harry said, "I am a black sheep. I never was so wicked till I went to war; my mother wets her pillow every night with her tears, on my account." I told him I was sorry, and hoped he would reform. Perhaps my advice availed but little, yet one thing I do know. Big Harry never said rough words in my house again. But in a short time Martha said, "Ma, just look at our sheep." I looked out, and saw our sheep running to the top of a hill near, then back on to the roof of a shed that was built against the foot of the hill; then they would run back again. One large sheep had old clothing fastened around his neck, and a heavy old oil cloth tied to one foot. I went out to the shed, and when the sheep ran near, I released the one from his frightful equipage. Then I went to the house and said, "I want a cane;" but not seeing one said, "I will go without." Then I went to the rail road shanty. There was plank seating, from the sides of the door, all around the inside of the room. This seating was fully ocupied by the workmen. Big Harry sat in the door. The men did not look up: some of them were smoking, and not one lifted his eyes from the floor, when I stepped near the door and said. "What have I done to cause offense? My sheep are easily frightened, and once were gone a long time on account of fright—I don't want them frightened any more. If I have done anything wrong, tell me what it is." Then I turned and walked toward our house. Big Harry got up from his seat and came round, saying, "Mrs. Murray, it was not me that done the mischief." But one of the masons told me that he saw him do it, and that he was in the fault; yet in my presence he was ever afterwards quite respectful. The third morning after, Big Harry and Jack were added to our list of boarders. Jack was missing; also a beautiful horse belonging to a poor laborer that lodged with the masons in our chamber. That poor laborer was very small of stature, and depended on his beautiful team, to help support a wife and seven children. The thief had borrowed money, borrowed a revolver, got pay for work before it was done, stole our saddle and bridle, and left the country. The poor laborer made what exertions he could to find his horse, but failed.

One day before Jack left, two men drove up,

came in and requested a meal; it was soon ready, and while they dined there was mischief outside of our dwelling. The men returned to their wagon that was left near our stable-yard, and not far from the railroad shanty. They had left two good overcoats, two blankets and a keg of cider vinegar on the wagon; all was missing and could not be found. The persons who had lost their property gave me their names on paper; and I told them I would inform them if I got any trace of the lost property. Some hours afterward, during the time of labor, our Martha walked up on the hill near our house, and back near a ravine; she saw something that frightened her. She returned to the house and said, "There is something on the ground; I do not know what it is." Miss Raynolds was at our house at the time; she accompanied Martha back, and they returned carrying two blankets. I showed them to some of the stone masons; they said, "They are the lost blankets." I sent word to the town of Peabody, the owners recovered them, and expressed many thanks to us for the same.

One morning the contractor, Mr Malady, had to leave the persons in his employ for a short time, for the purpose of drawing their pay. Then part of those persons belonging to the shanty, thought they would have a jubilee; they came in a crowd to my back door, and on the outside of the dwelling they placed seats; and when seated commenced to sing. Then they would shout, clap their hands and say, "Glory hallelujah!" then sing again. I said nothing, but merely closed the door. Soon some one said to them, "Mr. Malady is coming!" then they scattered quickly to their own quarters.

But as we consider the ways of the wicked, the language of the inspired apostle Paul meets the case in consideration: "Despisest thou the riches of His goodness, and forbearance and long-suffering, not knowing that the goodness of God leadeth thee to repentance; but after thy hardness and impenitent heart, treasurest up unto thyself wrath, against the day of wrath, and revelation of the righteous judgement of God, who will render to every man according to his deeds."

CHAPTER LXXIX. A TEXAN RUFFIANS AT NEWTON.

Mr. Mulally paid off his workmen, and I heard him tell the stone masons not to leave my house till Big Harry left. He said, "I fear Harry might do some harm." The common workmen left immediately, and soon every one had taken their departure.

Then Martha and I were left alone. Toward evening a man drove round near the house and alighted. I did not think his appearance indicated any good; therefore prevented his entering the house. He demanded money. I told him, "Your horses are going to run off." He stepped a little toward them, and when he turned again, I had taken a strong green stick in hand, which was near by, and told him I had no money for him, but had many expenses to meet; and if he stepped one step toward me, he would be sorry. I stood with the stick raised; then he said, "I am a Texan. I am a ——. I can get sins pardoned. What are you?" I told him, "You will find out to your sorrow, if you step one step this way." Just then his horses started, and ran a little distance into a fence; he started after them; then after a few threatening words, left the premises.

God could have worked a miracle for our protection, but I feel thankful that he gave the necessary energy, that kept that wicked person from crimes of deeper wrong.

We were a little fearful of his return, and were much on our guard. About three days afterwards he passed our house, partially intoxicated, and driving two horses, which he had stolen; but he was not seen on our streets afterwards.

The wicked flee when no one pursueth, and the fear of the Lord is to hate evil; yet there are some who turn judgement into wormwood, and leave off righteousness on the earth; still they are commanded to seek Him that made the Seven Stars and Orion; and turneth the shadow of death into the morning; the Lord, is his name.

After the rail road had been worked through past our home the distance of twenty-five or thirty miles, there was a delay in the prosecution of the work; a town called Newton being for a time the termination of the road, it became for that period a rendezvous for the ruffians of society. Men were daily shot down on the streets, either for the purpose of robbery or hate. Officers were powerless to suppress the riot and crime, till at last soldiers were sent to maintain the peace. I kept my front door and windows locked during the day, and had my house closely secured at night. We often saw Mexicans, Texans, Negroes and cattle drovers passing. Therefore we thought carefullness and preparation for self-defense, was both advisable and commendable.*

---

*Lone woman cannot be too careful or heroic, in guarding her honor and rights. A lack in that respect would be no merit.

There were many persons coming into our country, who were destitute of the principles of right; and our corn-cribs and chicken-roosts often told stories of robbery or depredation.

CHAPTER LXXX.—AN IMPRESSION, A SOUND, A SKELETON.

One afternoon I told Martha, I felt sure something was going to be wrong, and requested her to secure a young horse near the house, saying, "It might be stolen before morning." She went and brought the animal near and drove the wooden pin to which his rope was fastened, very tightly in the ground.

After committing ourselves into the care of Providence, as the shades of a moonlight evening were resting on the face of nature, I retired to my couch, but not to sleep. After a little time, I heard the picket that secured the colt, knocked out of the ground. I waked Martha and told her what I heard. We then went to a window and looked out on the beautiful moonlight, and saw that the colt was gone. We retired to our couch, but remained for some time talking and thinking of what had happened. After remaining for a time wakeful, I heard sounds like some person in distress, and terror. Soon as day dawned, Martha and I started up the valley, and saw the colt come draging his lariet.

The grass on the prairie was large and becoming dry and soon was burnt off by prairie fire. One day I was riding up the valley, and overtook a neighbor; he pointed a little from the road, saying, "I found a dead man there yesterday; I went to talk with those persons working in that stone quarry near, and saw something that looked singular; we all went to look, and found the frame of a man, still laying in his clothing." After hearing this, I rode to the town of Florence on the railroad, two miles and a half from our house. On my return I went and looked closely at the skeleton, a few rods from the road-side. A blue checked shirt, a gray coat with one sleeve torn off, partially concealing the skeleton; the hair of the head still laying by the skull, one boot covering a perished limb; a wolf or something of the kind had pulled one boot aside.

After these observations, when I had just passed the place where murder had been transacted, two doctors from the town of Florence, arrived and carefully examined the skeleton, then placed it, and the clothing with it, in a box, and returned to Florence.

The doctors said, "The man had been shot in the head, and had a blow also that had broken some of his face bones." Between where the skeleton lay and the road-side, was found the sleeve that had been torn from the murdered man's coat, his hat and a quilt, was identified as belonging to a traveler, who was no doubt returning in a carriage in which he traveled, but never arrived at his home. The clothing and down grass must have been wet and therefore did not burn when the prairie grass round was consumed.

The written word of God declares: "The dark corners of the earth are full of the habitations of cruelty;" and "no murderer hath eternal life abiding in him." Satan was a murderer from the beginning, and Cain slew his brother, because he was more righteous than himself.

What a happy change would be in this fallen world, if the love of God ruled in every heart. But oh! what devastation and crime has the prince of the powers of darkness accomplished by his agencies.

CHAPTER LXXXI.—TRIALS, HOUSE IN FLAMES.

Trials and afflictions were on every hand. I could not always get to Church as formerly on account of rheumatic affliction, but when I could ride to the place of worship, it was ever esteemed a privilege to meet with those who worship God in spirit and in truth, and when rising in the morning of each day, I opened my Bible and bowed before God, asking the Divine teaching of God's Holy Spirit and felt the consolations of the same. I was afflicted with neuralgia for several years, and the circumstances of the death of my dear Mary, rested heavily upon my mind. Other trials, which I will not mention, but leave with God, robbed me of earthly comfort.

One extremely cold day the wind and snow was sweeping round; a man at the gate called out, "I am freezing, can I get into the house?" I opened the gate, he came in, I made a warm fire. After he had warmed thoroughly, and wrapped well, he started on his journey. Martha was in the sitting room knitting. After the traveler had left, she called out, "Mother I heard something fall in the chamber." I supposed it was some trifling event, and still continued my domestic affairs. Soon Martha said, "I hear fire cracking and burning—the house is in flames." Martha carried a ladder to the back of the house; our well was near. I got water and ascended the ladder; I could walk on the roof of the kitchen, but could not walk on the roof of the main building, and carry water. I dashed water on the fire, but it would run and unite again. Martha brought water several times, but I soon saw there must be a change in our operations; there never could have been more rapid work performed, than what was accomplished at that time.

We could not get the ladder up our stairway; I set it against the house, ran up stairs, gave the sash of a window such a jerk, that the side strip which held the sash, broke into three pieces. The window being out, I drew the ladder into the chamber, shoved it up through the burning roof, and mounted upon it, surrounded by consuming flames. Martha more rapidly than would scarcely be imagined, drew and brought me water. We had two buckets, and a half gallon cup. There was no human being in the sound of our voice: we knew that all depended on our speedy exertions, and the help of Providence.

Once some clothing in the chamber was near being consumed by fire falling from the burning roof. I threw water on them, and hastily turned a bed one side, and continued to contend with the flames. I said, "Martha, if we see that we cannot extinguish the flames, we will secure those things that are most valuable in the dwelling." But we still worked on, and I prayed, "Oh! heavenly Father, help me; Thou hast helped me in days past; Thou canst help now; Thou hast promised to help Thy children when they call upon Thee; Thy word must stand." While I prayed and still battled with the flames, they raised less high, and soon were extinguished. Then our plight was more comical than desirable, for my hair was down, and hung in icicles; my sleeves were wet and frozen. I had taken off my shoes to walk on the roof, and my stockings were frozen to my feet. Martha had carried water up stairs so rapidly, that much of her clothing was wet and frozen. But soon comfort was restored and real thankfulness to God took possession of our minds.

God has said in the 91 Psalm, 15 verse, "Call upon me and I will answer." He will be with His people in time of trouble, and deliver them. His word is truth, and though His children may often be surrounded by danger and trials, yet God never forgets for one moment, His lowliest child that trusts in Him.

God often moves in a mysterious way,
His wonders to perform.
The bud may have a bitter taste,
Yet sweet will be the flower.
What we know not now, eternity will reveal.

CHAPTER LXXXII.--AN ABSENT SON. FREEZING TO DEATH.

Nearly all the settlers on our side of the Cottonwood river, were French people from Florence, down the valley for some miles. Several small streams that emptied into the Cottonwood, were settled exclusively by French and were mostly Catholics.

My boy was out near the great bend of the Arkansas, or somewhere near the south-west part of Kansas, on the buffalo ground nearly three months. I heard that several persons had frozen to death in that direction, and from some accounts I thought most likely, my son had shared a similar fate. One of our neighbors was brought home dead; he had frozen to death while the crossing prairie. His son who was with him was so near frozen that he lost part of his feet, and all his fingers.

I heard nothing certain from my boy, and in stillness of the night, the clock bell would sound as a death knell, speaking of a lost, lost son. One evening two young men called, and said, "We are very hungry." I gave them what I had prepared. They expressed their thanks, and said, "If possible in the future, they would be glad to reward me for the food I gave them." Then I remarked, I had done by them just as I would wish others to do by an absent son of mine, for whom I felt much solicitude; they looked sorrowful and left our home, but when all was stillness around, and the cheerful sunshine was striving to make all nature smile, my boy entered our home. He regretted much his absence, and said, "If I had come home and found our house burnt down, I would have felt very bad." Shall I dwell on the many trials that marked my pathway? Oh! no, surely not, for all things shall work together for good, in regard to those who love God. Our light afflictions, which are but for a moment work out for us a far more exceeding and eternal weight of glory. Yet we read that the wicked rob the widow and the fatherless. Wickedness stalks abroad in the land, to draw the young and unsuspected, into the snares of Satan. And how many parents' hearts have been wrung with anguish, when they have beheld dear ones that have been more precious to them than their own lives, whom they have taught to choose the path of piety and peace, by the luring smiles of a deceitful world, unconsciously drawn near the whirlpool of distruction.

Dear youth who may these pages read, for the sake of your own best interest, in time and eternity, like king Solomon, ask God to give you wisdom, that your steps in life, may be guided thereby. God giveth liberally and upbraideth not. May you never have to repent, that you have bartered a pure conscience and youthful advantages, for a mess of pottage.

Dear youthful friend, ever shun temptation; ask help of the strong arm of Omnipotence; keep a conscience pure, and when this fleeting life is ore, may the bright realms of glory, and the melody of the ransomed, be yet more increased by the addition of your immortal being.

CHAPTER LXXXIII.— GRASSHOPPERS. LOSSES, A VISIT, OUR RELATIVES. A TERRIBLE VISITATION, A DYING CHARGE, AN ACQUAINTANCE.

September 14, 1874.

William Murray, though a mere youth, was married to Miss Laura Jane Joseph. They remained with me much of the time, but the summer previous was very dry, and grasshoppers had been very destructive. My son had met with several losses; our land tax had been very extortionary, and I had no income; our stock had been sold to pay taxes, and my family was in need of help. A tract of land was sold at low figures, squaring all debt, and rendering necessary assistance. A portion of the price remained unpaid till the following year, Febuary, 1875.

I thought best to visit the home of a brother-inlaw, Mr. Hanson Murray. I started on the cars, from Florence, Marion Co., Kansas, taking my daughter Martha with me, to visit her uncle, aunt and cousins, who resided in Holt Co., Missouri. I left my son and his wife in charge of our home; and the cars rolled onward, till we arrived at Forbs Station, Holt Co., Missouri. We were met, as we stepped from the cars upon the platform by Mr. Linville Murray, a cousin to Martha, though her senior, and were soon introduced to his daughter Anna, a lovely young lady about the age of Martha, and were by them conducted to their residence, where we met for the first time with the excellent lady, Mrs. Mary Linville Murray, and were soon met by many other dear friends, and made very welcome by all.

Brother Hanson Murray was lingering on the shores of time, while consumption preyed upon his vitals. He was the last of five brothers, to bid adieu to earth. This brother of my departed companion, had long been numbered with the people of God on earth, and oh! how blessed the joyful foretaste of heaven on this side Jordan's flood, when God is all and in all to us. Our brother was waiting to join the general assembly, and Church of the first born in heaven. His numerous family was married, with the exception of a younger daughter, and all were trying to live, so that they might at last meet their Father in the new Jerusalem, where affliction and death, never can disturb the holy joy of the ransomed.

Prayer meeting was often held in the dwelling of the afflicted one, and once when I and my daughter were present. Eight of his children, four sons and four daughters, and their companions, his wife and their grand children were present. After the meeting had been duely opened by reading the Word of God, singing and prayer, the brother ready to cross the river of death, gave each of his relatives, and the companions of his children, a separate council, and what we all considered his dying charge. There was much weeping, and deep solemnity; a scene not easily forgotten by any present, yet the Father remained for some time, waiting and desiring his home in heaven.

I was in that community about five months, and took charge of a Sabbath-school class of young ladies; and am much indebted to the different branches of the family of Bro. H. Murray, for their kindness to their aunt and cousin, during our stay among them.

A young man attended meetings and Sabbath-school in their community, of piety and prominence. That young man and Martha, formed an acquaintance which was lasting.

My son wrote for me to come home; his family were not in good health. Soon as I could make arrangements for our departure, we complied with the request. But ere we left, we learned a sad account of one who was a resident of Holt Co., and who bore a disfigured appearance. He was once seated in a saloon, with three other persons. They were all engaged in playing cards, in the time of a thunder storm; and when the lightning flashed vividly, and the thunder roared loudly, those wicked men blasphemously dared the Almighty God, to come and play cards with them. Immediately a current of electricity entered the saloon, forced a barrel of whisky against the door, and set the whisky on fire. Three of the card players were consumed by those flames, one broke his way through the window, and plunged into the Missouri river, whose waters rolled near by; thus extinguishing the fire that had kindled upon his person, and thus protracted his existence. That poor mortal thought as he had a day of grace yet left, he had better prepare to stand before his Judge, and break off his sins by righteousness, and his iniquities by turning to the Lord. He desired the prayers of those who had an interest in a throne of grace, and requested that his name should be placed on the Church list.

Though God bears long with the wicked, yet the inspired writer tells us in the Book of Divine truth, God has bent His bow, and made it ready, and judgment against sinners, and justice may not long slumber.

I will here speak of another incident that came under our notice, of one who was hardened in sin, and dared the God who holds the elements in His control, to try the same on him; and soon he was laid a blackened corpse on the ground.

The wicked may say, God will not visit all with speedy judgment. Yet, O presume not to sin, but fly quickly to Christ; no longer grieve His word. He cries,

    How can I give Thee up,
    Or let the lifted thunder drop.

CHAPTER LXXXIV.—AN ADIEU, KANSAS HOME.

Now let us look round upon the faces of our kind friends, before we start on our journey to western Kansas. Martha let us go once more into those orchards. The apples hanging there on their native stem, you say, is "a curiosity" to you. In our western country, in those early days, more care was taken for the growth of wheat or stock, than for those healthy delicacies of life. Fruit surely is among the choice blessings of Providence, and no pains should be spared in the cultivation of the same. Those fragrant sweet roses, and nice pinks in bloom, how sweet.

Prairie flowers bloom in western lands. One sweet ball of flowers with fragrance rare and leaves surpassing art, I have seen upon those western hills: those flowers possessed modest worth; their name was sensative.

Now dear brother, we your home must leave, and shortly you a home in heaven will gain, which Christ has gone before us to prepare. May the dear ones, you leave on this side the valley, you are about to enter, be blessed in time and eternity; and may you be permitted with holy ones on the shining shore, to sound a more melodious strain of joy, as each happy traveller arrives within the golded gates of the New Jerusalem.

But I must say to all and each, what to us seems a long adieu. Mary Linville, and Anna standing by your side, your face full of real sincere kindness; sweet lovely sister, I must say farewell. After many good wishes and parting words, we found ourselves gliding on toward our Kansas home. When there arrived, I met my only son and his wife. That evening God's Word was read within our dwelling, prayer ascended in deep sincerity to a throne of mercy.

Martha held correspondence by letter with William A. Parker, of her acquaintance in the state of Missouri; they were engaged to be married. Time rolled onward.

William Murray called a son his own; some weeks passed, and he moved his family to the town of Florence. Poor William: I remember you with a mother's sympathy. Your slender constitution, your many loses; and the serious accidents you have met, doth your health affect; but oh! the soul is more than all. Jesus waiting stands and shows His bleeding hands; he will sins forgive, and wash you white as snow. Oh! trust in Jesus' name and own His cause; then you can sing of a home in heaven, where toil is o'er, and sorrow never shall come. Oh! do not despond, but rise with firmness and manhood. Resist all evil in the strength of your Redeemer;

and may God bless you and your companion with all things for your greatest good, both spiritual and temporal.

CHAPTER LXXXV.—ALONE AGAIN. HEROISM, UNCIVILITY.

Martha and I were again alone, and our circumstances caused Martha to exert herself far more than girls generally do. The water in our well had failed; I employed two men to dig it deeper. Martha loaded and hauled the rock, to build the extra wall. Those persons we employed, promised they would chop and haul wood, and take wheat which I had on hand, as recompense for their work, but they did not return. All the down wood on our land, had been hauled off without our knowing the extent of our loss, until I attended Martha to the grove. Then the girl with resolute heroism, sharpened her ax, and chopped down stately trees, loaded the heavy green wood on a wagon, hauled it from the opposite side of the Cottonwood stream, and chopped the wood right size for our stove, when near the door.

Thus throughout the later season of the fall, and through the winter, till the latter part of the month of February, she got the fuel for our fire.

In the fall about the latter part of October, when Martha and I were all the occupants of our home; one moonlight night, about the hour of eleven, when I was wakeful on my couch, a very heavy rap was heard on the door. I hastily waked Martha; we rose and placed more garments about our person. I stepped near a window, and under a curtain, looked out through the moon-beams on a portico, and saw two strangers. Martha and I thought those persons much out of place. We had rods, and each with determination held one. The heavy raps continued; we kept silent. Soon one said, "You had better open this door; you are in their; we saw you when we passed the house before night, and this door will be opened quick." I stepped near the door, and said, "If you break this door, you will be sorry; we are prepared, and will teach you better manners." Then he said, "Our team is sick. We want a book, your neighbor C. says you have got in the house." I said, "We don't open our door at this late hour; but if you will stand out away from the house that we may see you in the moonlight. I will put the book out of the house." Soon as this was done, I unlocked a window and dropped the book out side; then when one came to pick it up, I said, "Don't you never treat lone women so very uncivil again. You ought to be ashamed of your uncivility.

They left without reply, and in the morning, soon as light of day appeared, Martha and I rode over to the house of neighbor C. There we found the persons who on our portico the night before had stood. There were two families present. I told before all in the house, how the young men had conducted, and said, "Mr. C., don't you never send persons to my house at such an hour. If they ever come in such a way again, they will repent of their course."

Mrs. C. told me; "One of the young men will lose the chance to wed his bride, if we report to the young lady, the ill manners he displayed last evening."

We hope he learned a lesson, to be remember for time to come.

CHAPTER LXXXVI.—SHE CHANGED HER NAME, PATRIMONY.

Near the close of the month of February, 1879, Mr. William Parker came two hundred miles, and soon after his arrival at our home, Miss Martha A. Murray, changed her name, to that of Mrs. Martha A. Parker.

But as I write, I stop, and out the window look upon the pleasant green. The sun looks now, with radience bright, from underneath a cloud. And nature smiles, while many trees all round, full bloom display. The spring time of the year, which nature crowns with grace is here; her velvet carpet spreads, and like an Eden seems.

Thus might the young and fair forever see, naught but flowers along their path; but cares will come. And though our youth may bear their part full well. Yet youth as well as aged ones, are often made to feel, there is nothing firm but heaven. Yet young friend, William Parker; you have sought God, and owned His name, morning and evening, you look within the sacred pages to read God's holy will; and bow around the family altar. Oh! may rays from the eternal throne, descend on your devoted souls, made one in Christ.

Now of my patrimony, let this suffice to say, as my children little had of earthly goods or treasures, I did my all of earthly worth on them bestow. I have since then thought of Christ, who became poor and left His Father's throne above, a rich inheritance for us to gain. And if the avaricious ones of earth, have wronged, or still may wrong my children dear, they will have to settle with the judge of all the earth.

To this subject, I will only add; our home in Marion Co., was sold, and now in Osage Co., Kansas, my children dwell; with the exception of a little grand child, who with her father resides in Marion Co.

CHAPTER LXXXVII.— AFFLICTIONS. CHANGE OF RESIDENCE.

The Winter and Spring of 1877, found the writer of these lines suffering extremely from rheumatic affliction in the left arm and shoulder.

I learned an extent of suffering in that respect, which I had scarcely imagined. But when the warm settled season of the year arrived, God blessed the use of means. I recovered strength, and through the summer of that year, I walked weekly, one and a half miles to the town of Melvern, Kansas, where I met with the people of God, to worship the Giver of all consolation that will stand, by heirs of immortality, amidst the changing vicisitudes of life.

I gladly heard the gospel dispensed, sitting under the droppings of the same. The Sabbath-school and singing at that place, was interesting. And when I heard the children sing, I thought of the words of inspiration. "The kingdoms of this world are become the kingdoms of our Lord and his Christ."

Late in the fall of 1877, it seemed Providence designed, there should be a change in my residence. The way was prepared, and bidding my son and his wife adieu, accompanied by my daughter and her companion, I was on the way to the cars at Williamsburg. I left Martha at the carriage. My son-in-law went into the car, and saw me take a seat. He spoke kind words and a parting adieu. "And now dear children all, may Christian love forever make its home with you, and of each others interests, and health take care. And while ambitious to save earthly stores, remember heaven."

CHAPTER LXXXVIII.—WITHIN THE CARS. OBSERVATION.*

*Chapter 88, was written in a car window.

Now within the cars I am seated.
My children's forms have faded from my view.
I feel a weakness, and can scarcely sit erect,
But must cheer up, and think on brighter things
Something more than parting.
The cars slowly moving at the first,
Then faster, faster, speed the way.
Through a window now, prairie level see.
Then rolling lands, vallys and groves.
Smaller streams, and mighty rivers,
Urge their way to the gulf below.
But we look and see small elevations rise,
Then height on height romantic, oft with groves adorned.
Or rocky summits rising clift ore clift,
And now a city's side,
Powerful waters rolling by, which have for ages flowed.
Now behold our mighty land, in her autumnal dress,
Dotted ore with enchanted domes, or humbler peasant's cot.

Within the village, or round the solid city walls,
Hear the busy active hum of human life.
The immortal mind, how vast, how great,
Behold the machinery of our day,
Employed both in the city and the field.
The cars adorned oft with beauty,
Moving swift at his command,
Who through a microscope might survey the stars,
And tell the revolutions of more worlds than ours.
By the telegraphic line with lightning speed,
He talks with friends or nations miles away.
The mind expands, and proves an origin immortal.
Yet greater still is the Creator, God,
Who holds the universe within His powerful sway.
But as we fly along, in the rushing cars,
Let us consider lesser things.
As we out the window look,
More less than real, each passing object doth appear:
See fencing, rock, hedge and plank,
Corn upon a thousand hills, ore many vallys too,
Great powerful God is Thine.
Cattle feeding on the plain,
And the noble horse at large, on pastures fair.
And stock condemned by Jewish laws, numberless enclosed.
See a mighty oak, stand lone on the plain.
Wind and storms, have added strength unto its growth.

Thus may our souls be more matured for heaven,
And when all things mortal, from our vision fades,
May our immortal souls have union with the Deity,
And joyful stand within the New Jerusalem.
And when before the great white throne,
The congregated millions stand,
May we behold a smiling Judge in Christ our Lord.
Yet while we linger here below,
May we follow according to Divine command.
Whatsoever things are pure and lovely.
Now of this soliloquy no more.
At Kansas City, we have arrived.
Here we take a through ticket for Chicago,
Enter a sleeping car, and on an easy seat reclined.
Swiftly the cars rolled on until the dawn of day.

CHAPTER LXXXIX.— A LADY, UNION FLAG, PENITENTIARY.

Then from a Station on the road, a Lady entered of kind and thoughtful mien, her conversation full of intelligence and plans of charity. As we passed a Penitentiary, she said: "Look quick, boys are there, with whom I have talked about their sins, they say "Sabbath breaking, evil companions, and strong Drink, have been their ruin." I talked with them of hope and reformation; they wept like children. One said, he would "ever do the right in time to come, and would ask God, (who delights to help and bless), for aid, through future days." Then this angel of mercy said: "Oh! how my heart aches for the wandering ones, who are drawn into Sin by evil influence." As we passed on, I looked on the dusky walls, and saw the Union Flag floating in the breeze, and thought: "Oh! If there was no sin, how this earth would be to an Eden changed," and here we remember a young man, who said: "Six years before that time, he was shot by one, who was under the influence of strong Drink." The wound had caused him much affliction and from that period he had been a Temperance Lecturer.

Sin stalks abroad and many victims fall,
Slain by the Serpents deadly power;
But let the dying Sinner look to Jesus,
For he is waiting to bestow the healing balm,
Which makes the Wounded whole
And cures the sin-sick Soul.
When mercy is free, and Jesus' Love so great,
Why will you turn away, Oh! Sinner come;
No longer grieve a God of Love,
And down to ruin run.

CHAPTER XC.—AT MOTHER'S HOME IN GOSHEN.

We now stop at Chicago and get a ticket for the place of our destination. On again toward Goshen, Elkhart Co., Indiana, we by an engines power are carried, and through God's mercy and preserving care: when there arrived, my mother and a sister I met on the platform. When a few days had passed, a brother, whom I had not seen for nineteen years, once more I met at my mother's home; and while before the Throne of Grace, we bowed in prayer, that brother, at the mercy seat, talked with God, and thanks were given for favours past, and mercy claimed for time to come. And at my mother's home, this pleasant Spring of 1878, I have penned these lines, and if beneficial, or do entertain, to God alone be all the praise.

CHAPTER XCI.—A JOURNEY.

A SUPPLEMENT.

When Pioneers in their onward journey hurried forward, two sisters, with joyous smiles and innocent glee, marched side by side, or by turns guided the reins of the useful steed, that drew the loaded wagons onward. As they tarried at a dwelling for rest, a young lady, lovely and refined in all her ways, displayed her library, and the conversation was elevating and poetical. But those young ladies, whose souls seemed as one for a few passing hours, could no more mingle in harmony of soul as one.

The Pioneers passed on to a western home, and as they went along the silent stream of Stillwater river, not a ruffle on the water, yet it looked forth in grandeur, as a noble work of the Creator, God. They commented, concerning the placid stream, but a sound broke on their ears. Then behold, circling waves, verging to a centre, round and round surged the edying waves, whirling, roaring, carrying all beneath the tunnel-formed waters.

The youth's paused, then passed on: but a second Whirlpool saluted their wondering gaze. Then they smiled to see whatever they saw fit to consign to the watery elements; whirl round and round, sink lower and lower, till lost in an unknown abyss.

But "where are those sisters now?" Ah! The edying wave of time has surged and whirled the rounds of thirty-two annual revolutions; but some of those travelers have not yet fathomed the verging goal. The oldest of those sisters, who walked along the green verdant banks of Stillwater, is the writer of this volume.—And in California, meeting trials and disappointments, dwells one, whose lovely face is pictured on the minds eye, in ligaments, never to be effaced. But if friends meet no more on earth, there is a point of time, when lost to mortal gaze the faithful soul ascends to God. There is a Divine power, far surpassing the wisdom of this world, that can lift the child of God, from seeming dissolution, to walk the paved streets of the New Jerusalem, and bathe in the Water of Life, and drink from the crystal fountain of Salvation and never fading Glory; while the boundless waves, shall usher continually, a more glorious crowning to the citizens of Zion.

The elder Pioneer, the father, who battled with the trials of life, has by those trials found a more speedy exit from earth. That father, who told his little girl the first she ever knew of Jesus, is at rest, and two noble brothers have met speedy exits down the verging waves; and the remains of another Pioneer, who passed more westward in company with myself, and three little ones, is resting beneath the sod in Kansas. Also a most lovely daughter has left the vain scenes of earth. But there will be a joyful meeting, when the waves of time have whirled their rounds a little longer; for truly, a journey of a day, is a picture of human life.

CHAPTER XCII.—NEW COUNTRY.

In country new, near bogy roads, ore swampy lands, where dense forests have demanded the wood-man's ax; pole-bridges have made the travelers journey, in an early day, more passable; and notwithstanding their roughness, they are sometimes a curiosity. Thirty-two years ere this time, when the loaded vehicles of a pioneer rolled over a pole-bridge. The bridge shook through the whole length of it, which was more than three quarters of a mile long; as though there were no tera-firma beneath it and was a fair representative of any thing, without a solid basis. And a great contrast to country, where dry Prairie meets the eye of the traveler, skirted with groves and clear rolling streams; yet the Creator has formed each portion of our America, having its own peculiar advantages.

CHAPTER XCIII.—THE RECKLESS.

When I was honored with citizen-ship in my Kansas home, a traveler called and I gave him food; he was a mere youth, but had wandered westward, far from his native roof. He said "in a dark corner of the earth, where cruelty and sin abounded, men's bones, where he had been, were bleeching on the ground."

I believe the traveler was honest in his declaration; he was employed for a time as a laborer in Florence, Kansas.

Again another traveler called, and when a repast was preparing, he said: "I spent last night in the new railroad town of Newton; there was only a thin partition between my room and a dying man, that had been shot in the evening by a desparado. The poor mortal, who was about to launch into eternity, uttered desperate oaths, as long as his fast-ebbing life would permit the words to flow. Oh! it was dreadful, such as I never want to hear again."

Thus spoke our guest, and I would add: "Let me not die the death of the wicked, and let not my last days be like theirs." I have heard the reckless boast, that "wicked out-laws, full of murder and revenge, have died without fear, and when they knew they were mortally wounded, have only thought of, and acted out revenge." Oh! how dreadful, thus to rush, as it were on Jehovah's bucler. No wonder, the ire of a Holy God would rest on the wicked, whom he will consume with the Spirit of His mouth, and with the brightness of His coming. "For God, out of Christ, is a consuming fire."

How dreadful for an immortal Being, to have the finer sensibilities of nature callous and dead, to right and truth. Lost, lost forever, from the society of those, who are clothed in fine linnen, clean and white, and who follow the Lamb, whithersoever he goeth; on whose triumphant banner will be inscribed: Victory, victory, glory immortal to God and the Lamb.

CHAPTER XCIV. VISITING THE SICK. RELIGION.

While walking along the banks of a rolling stream, seven wolves, an old one and six nearly grown, were started quickly in my path-way and skulking hide or swim the stream and on an oasis stop. From a fountain I dipped a sparkling draught, and as I homeward turned, saw a wild-cat watch me from a bush; but hastening onward, found a traveler at my home, who said, "With the consumption a lady expects soon to die. She has no joy or hope of heaven. No one to tell her what to do. Will you please to go and tell her what you know of a Christian's hope and heaven. She has expressed a wish to see you, and sent this request.

Although the lady lived ten miles away in Marion Center, those miles were quickly passed on horse-back; and by the couch of Mrs. C. Billings, we talked of Him who wept at the grave of Lazarus. The sympathizing friend who loved a fallen world, and gave Himself to die, that He might bring our wayward souls, to eternal life in heaven. The afflicted one recovered for a time, and was faithful to her vows. Though now, she has gone to brighter realms, to hear the angels sing, and clothed in garments white, with heavenly glorious light. Behold her Lord and King.

I will tell you of another lady, who lived seven miles from my home in Kansas. Once she sent a man to tell me to come and see her. I could not go that day, but soon went. When I entered her dwelling, I found her sick on her bed. Then she said, "Why did you not come quick; I thought I was going to die, and could not, till I had seen you; but now I am better, and shall get well." I told her if you please we will read a little in my Testament, and then we will pray. She assented, and when we rose from prayer she said, "You don't pray like we do. We pray to the Father, Son and Mary. Once when I was sick, a priest had me swallow a little God."

I had more than once lamented this woman's dark state of soul, and tried to hold the light of truth before her mind. But she thought she would get well, and served mammon all she could. One day I met her, and she said, "Mrs. Murray, the old Boy will get me. I swear; I get very mad; the old Boy will have me after a little." I told her to ask God to help her stop sinning. Then she said, "I keep and image hanging by my bed, and look at it very often. I have another in my trunk; it is nice, and wrapped with gause. I often look to it. You belive your way, and I will mine."

Again we met, and ere she saw me, I heard

such oaths, as I never before heard a woman speak. But when she looked round, she said, "The priest has been here, and I will try to be a better Catholic."

Once more we met. Then she said, "I am toiling all the time, and after a while I will have to die, and leave the riches I have got; we have no children, and who will get what I have accumulated." I said, Mrs. B., would it not be nice to know how long you would live, and make use of some of your riches for your comfort at least. She said, "Yes, spend what I have got, and then they would say, one big fool at last."

I left her never to meet on earth again. But in eternity who will be the wise (that shall shine as the sun in the kingdom of their Father,) but those who trust in a Triune God; the Almighty Father, who was in Christ His well beloved Son: reconciling a fallen world unto Himself, and the Holy Spirit, sent from God to bring us near to Him, before whom the angels bow, while bliss unutterable, each holy being fills. The blessed Spirit, the Holy Comforter can cheer His children with sweeter joys than earth can give, even though they may be surrounded by floods and flames of tribulation. Soon the Archangel's trump shall sound, and the echo, "Time shall be no longer;" rend the vaulted skies. A smiling Judge, most glorious, the ransomed ones shall meet. But oh! the text in God's Holy Book, let every sinner read, "God out of Christ is a consuming fire." God cannot look upon sin, with the least degree of allowance: "Therefore let us flee from sin, as from deadly poison, and by true and living faith in the Son of God, may our souls be made white as the light. Saved now and ever filled with all the sweetness of the Gospel, sit at the feet of Jesus, and when the books are opened at the great day of general assizes, our souls shall appear in all the beauty and purity of the ransomed.

> Christ bids the guilty now draw near;
> Repent, believe, dismiss your fear.
> Hark, hark, what precious words I hear.
> Mercy is free, mercy is free.
>
> And when the vale of death, I've passed;
> When lodged above the stormy blast,
> I'll sing, while endless ages last.
> Mercy was free, mercy was free.
>   Hallelujah! hallelujah! Amen.

CHAPTER XCV.—THE PRAYER OF FAITH.

There was a time of extreme drouth in Kansas. It seemed that all vegetation would soon perish from the drying rays of mid-summer. Even dews failed to refresh the thirsty land.

The time rolled round for a quarterly meeting at Cedar Grove, four miles from our dwelling. I filled the position of steward, and soon met the servants of God, at the place appointed for worship. Eld. Rice presided at the meetings. Soon after I met him, he remarked, "It appears to me that there is not a spark of real piety, for the distance of twenty-five miles east of this." And in a sermon the next Sabbath morning, he remarked, "There has not one of you been praying for rain." Then he read from the Bible, "Ask of Me the early and latter rain." And after a very definite, sound and devout address delivered in his own peculiarly solemn and impressive manner, the congregation bowed in worship, while the elder gave utterance to prayer full of faith and power.

In the afternoon of that day, when persons were collecting for service, they were compelled to hasten their steps, for abundance of rain commenced to fall, and although in the former part of the day, not a cloud was seen; yet at the close of the afternoon service, the water was standing in pools along the side of the street. But as we walked from the house of worship, one who had no thankful spirit, said, "I don't like that preacher; he prayed for rain, and there is not rain enough yet." But that night the face of nature was in a manner deluged by an unusual sweeping rain. The vines and gardens were revived, and comfort and nourishment afforded to many of the human family. The cause of God was honored by His faithful servant, whom God saw fit to honor.

The prophet Elias prayed earnestly that it should not rain, and it rained not on the earth for the space of three years and six months; and he prayed again, and the heavens gave rain, and the earth yielded her increase.

CHAPTER XCVI.— A GUIDE.

Children need the care of earthly parents; much more we need the presence and help of our heavenly Father.

I will mention an incident for illustration. When passing homeward from a place of worship, in company with a child, our rout lay across prairie land; suddenly a mirage appeared before us. My child said, "It seems as though we would soon go into a lake of water; what shall we do." I quieted his fears, telling him, "It is only a deceitful mirage, fear not, we are on a well known path." But not till we could view the groves near our home, did the deception pass away. If my child had been alone, he would have fled from the right path, and wandered from his home. And if Jesus does not guide us in the journey of life, we will wander in paths of sin, gain much harm, and lose heaven. But if Jesus is with us how cheering the prospect; though floods of tribulation lie in our pathway, we shall be guided safely and securely beyond the trials of a deceitful world. Without Jesus, the soul is dark and blind; but with Jesus for our friend, the Holy Spirit our guide, God can fill our souls with joy unspeakable, and full of glory, though tried like Paul and Silas, who sung praises to God in prison. No angels arm had power to redeem a lost world. God alone could pay the price of our redemption; he saw our lost estate, and infinite love arranged the plan.

> He left the shining seats above;
> Entered the grave in mortal flesh,
> And dwelt among the dead.

Jesus told His followers: "Lo I am with you always, even to the end of the world." The Holy Ghost can give power to His servants, and access to the heart of the wayward, and solid peace and joy to the humble child of God. Jesus has conquered death, and if the natural enmity of the human heart to God is changed to a fullness of heavenly love; so that we love God with all the soul mind and strength. Then we can say triumphantly,

> "Oh death, where is thy sting,
> Oh grave, where is thy victory."

And we well might feel, it would be better to depart from this mortal life, and put on immortality dwelling in the effulgence of that unuterable glory that awaits us.

> I know I am nearing the holy ranks,
>   Of friends and kindred dear;
> For I brush the dews on Jordan's banks;
>   The crossing must be near,

Oh! come angel bands;
 Come and around me stand.
Oh! bear me away on your snowy wings,
 To my eternal home.

I've almost gained my heavenly home;
 My spirit loudly sings;
The holy ones, behold they come;
 I hear the noise of wings.

 Oh! come angel bands, etc.

Oh! bear my longing heart to Him
 Who bled and died for me;
Whose blood now cleanses from all sin,
 And gives me victory.

 Oh! come angel bands, etc.

ADDITIONAL.

―――o―――

The author of this volume was born March 3, 1826. She was from earliest childhood the subject of religious impressions. At the age of nine years, her name was placed on the church-list. Jesus revealed Himself to her as a glorious Friend and Redeemer. Love to Jesus surpassed all earthly things in her estimation. Tears of love and joy often bedewed her face, while contemplating the love of the dear Saviour. The world with its allurements strove to draw her in its train, but Jesus' love was more powerful and precious.

When about the age of eighteen, God gave the power to believe and confess Jesus, an all sufficient Saviour, saving from all sin, sanctifying the soul, by faith in the dear Redeemer. From the very bottom of her soul she cried: "I will, I do believe" and after a little patient waiting and presistent faith, God sent the Holy Ghost with sealing power, and gave the assurance, that not anything should separate her from the love of God in Christ Jesus.

About that time, God brought many of the Youth's, who had been taught by her in school, to the knowledge of His saving power. Being naturally of an extremely retiring disposition, a desire to do the will of God, under the influence of divine teaching, was the propelling motive, to action in the service of her Redeemer. Christ was pursecuted and His faithful servants will be also, and if the adversary of souls can block the wheels of salvation, He is ready for that deed: but God will not forsake or forget his little ones. God cared for, and watched over Mrs. Murray in all afflictions, dangers, and trials; gave her a missionary work to do in the West, made her indeed a friend to afflicted ones, who were far from the aid of physicians; and caused her to promulgate the Gospel, for the relief of thirsting, sin sick souls.

She well knew, what mortal sufferings and physicial weakness meant, and therefore could smypathize with the afflicted. But God in His wisdom saw fit, that worldly treasures and hopes should perish; that he might draw his little one nearer to Himself, and fulfill all His own good will.

After a sojourn of eighteen years in Kansas, through the providence of God, Mrs. Murray returned to Goshen, Indiana; and now, as the evening of life is approaching, she waits the directing of her heavenly Guide, and shall be watching for the brightest star that ever rose in the moral horizon, to guide her to the unclouded Light of Immortal day.

LOVINA.

A DAILY FORM OF COVENANT.

Blessed Father, loving Jesus, Holy Spirit, I give my body and soul into Thy hands, have Thy whole Will on me; use me for Thy glory, and never let me grieve Thy spirit. I will be Thine every moment and all Thou art is mine; may I be Thine forever. I give myself to Thee, give Thyself to me. Father, I reverence Thy majesty and sink before Thee. Thou art a holy God, I submit my all to Thee. I live under Thy inspection and wonder at Thy glory. Blessed Jesus, Thou art my constant friend and companion, Thou art always with me. I can talk to Thee my meditor; Thou showest me the Father and my soul is filled with what I call glory. Thou takest me out and bringest me in. Thou art ever with me; Thou art my continual help. Holy Spirit, Thou art my comforter; I feel from Thy blessed influence a continual flame of holy love. I pray by Thy power, through Thee I am brought to Jesus, through Jesus I am brought to the Father, and in the Father I am lost, swallowed up in what I call glory; and I can say, glory be to the Father, glory be to the Son, and glory be to the Holy Spirit. I have union with the Trinity, thus: I see the Son through the Spirit, I find the Father through the Son, and God is my all in all. Amen and Amen.

www.ingramcontent.com/pod-product-compliance
Lightning Source LLC
Chambersburg PA
CBHW031944230426
43672CB00010B/2040